UNHOOKED

UNHOOKED

JAMES R. ADAIR, EDITOR

BAKER BOOK HOUSE
Grand Rapids, Michigan 49506

Copyright © 1971 by Baker Book House Company, Grand Rapids, Michigan 49506

*Standard Book Numbers: 8010-0017-3, paper;
8010-0018-1, cloth*

Library of Congress Card Catalog Number: 71-152901

Acknowledgment is made to Scripture Press Publications, Inc., Wheaton, Illinois, for permission to reprint the following stories (with adaptations in some instances) from its three Power/line *Sunday School take-home papers —* Power for Living, Power Life, *and* Young Teen Power: *"Quest for Love," "Breakaway," "George Balla's Last Great Trip," "I Was the Pushers' Plaything," "Cough Syrup: My Downfall," "Hooked on My On Medicine," "Speed Way to Destruction," "Instant Everything," "Step by Step — Down," and "Just One More."*

Printed in the United States of America

PREFACE

Because the personal stories in *Unhooked* are so representative of the life stories of many of the young people with whom we work in our Teen Challenge Centers, I feel as if I know each one. I have seen their broken hearts, their desperation, their search for that which truly and lastingly satisfies. I know of the depths of degradation to which they had sunk because of drug addiction. But I also know of the joy they experienced when they found Christ to be the answer to their problems. I've seen many lives, just as scarred as theirs, transformed by the renewing work of the Holy Spirit.

That's why I am very happy to see these stories in book form. Although to some, especially the drug addict himself, they may be hardly believable, from my personal experience, I know that God *can* reach down and transform the life of the most hardened addict.

From my reading of these fast-moving stories, one thing stands out. I am reminded again that no class, no neighborhood, no family, even no Christian family, is immune to the curse of drug addiction. The fact that the homes from which some of these young people came were Christian homes reinforces the fact that we parents must work at being both *Christians* and *effective parents.*

This is an exciting book for teens and parents alike. It will make them acutely aware of a problem that is reaching the epidemic stage. Hopefully, it will dissuade many from drug experimentation. I am certain it will be especially helpful in convincing the young person who is already hooked on drugs that there is a Way to become unhooked.

David Wilkerson

CONTENTS

Letter from an Addict 9

The Tragedy of the Hooked 13

1. From Off the Desert 21
   by Miriam Schultz

2. Cough Syrup: My Downfall 30
   by John Morgan as told to James R. Adair

3. Suicide Was My Solution 36
   by Domingo Garcia as told to Muriel Larson

4. I Was the Pushers' Plaything 42
   by Paddy Duncan as told to Monte C. Unger

5. Disc Jockey on a New Trip 50
   by James R. Adair

6. George Balla's Last Great Trip 59
   by Betty Swinford

7. Breakaway 66
   by Lon Gregg as told to James R. Adair and Stanley Baldwin

8. Quest for Love 77
   by Vicky Riccardella as told to James R. Adair and Charlene Blanchard

9. Monkey Off My Back 87
   by Herb Green

10. For Better — For Sure 94
    by Esther Indelicato

11. Hooked on My Own Medicine 100
    by Howard Thomas, M.D.

12. In from the Cold 108
    by Louis Angel Garcia

13. Thanks to Wendy's Mom 116
    by Inmate No. M-0069, State Correctional Institution at Dallas, Penn.

14. Instant Everything 119
    by Nina Walter

15. Speed Way to Destruction 122
    by Jani Jansen

16. Step by Step — Down 130
    as told to Dorothy Grunbock Johnston

17. Just One More 136
    by Parker Rice as told to Muriel Larson

    How to Spot a Drug User 142

    Help for Addicts 149

    About Some of the Words Used in This Book 155

LETTER FROM AN ADDICT

He was eighteen, clean-cut, popular — had a million friends, his mother said. He was a fabulous swimmer and skin diver, and so patriotic that he wanted to join the Air Force and condemned campus riots and draft card burners.

But somewhere along the line he got hold of drugs. Maybe it was just an experiment or two at first. But he got hooked. Once he thought he had conquered this problem. But after he left home to study aviation at a school in Texas, the old habit returned — and he was asked to leave after just six weeks.

In late 1970 he wrote this letter:

"TO OTHER YOUNG PEOPLE — I have used all types of drugs from hash, pot, acid to hard stuff. It's all a bad scene. The people who push it don't use it because they know it's bad stuff. They can see what it does to you. All you are doing is ruining your life and letting people make money through you. They are only using you.

"Drugs suppress, depress, dull your ability to function right. But most of all they kill and destroy. Not all tabs of acid are alike. Each tab has a different amount of acid in it. No two are alike. Also, no two vials or packages of heroin are the

10 • UNHOOKED

same. If you shoot up with a friend, chances are you're both on the same kind of a trip. You may both come down but in different worlds. Then again you may come down OK, while your friend is coming down, crashing bad.

"If you are crashing now or on a trip, remember, what are you going to get out of it? You're only destroying.

"Where are you going to go from pot — hash — acid — heroin?

"Man, if you are on the stuff, please — for your sake — get off it. If you can't fight it by yourself, then get help from someone. It may be rough, trying to straighten yourself out, but it's never too late.

"Man, at least try. That's not too much to ask. You don't know me, but I want to help because I needed help and someone helped me. There are a lot of real things to do, so many useful things we could do, and life offers only a short time in which to do it.

"I remember the words from a song, 'So much of life ahead, we have only just begun to live.' If you can kick drugs, then you will find out what the song is really about. Don't give up on your problems and escape by using drugs. It only makes more problems.

"I have ruined a part of my life that can never be repaired and have taken the chance of ruining myself for good. I finally found out the truth about drugs and have quit. If you quit, a whole new world of life can open up to you.

"If someone offers you drugs, be more of a man than I was and say No. Learn from my mistakes. I don't want anyone to go through the hell I went

Letter from an Addict • 11

through, and am still going through. These friends of yours will offer stuff free, then start making you pay for it.

"Then they sell you harder stuff at discount prices, then boost the prices up when they get you hooked. Remember the same person or friend who has grass will also be able to push heroin to you, and for what? To make money for himself while he destroys you. People who push are the ones who want to destroy you, and if you give them the chance they will.

"Please, if you need help get it.

"I have decided to take a trip better than drugs could ever offer. 'Life.' It's a great trip; try it before it's too late. Remember you can make life what it can be or something it should have been."

Something happened after he finished the letter. Nobody knows exactly why he did it. It could easily be that drugs had affected his mind. Or maybe suddenly he felt he would never have the power to take that great trip called "Life." Whatever the reason, he turned on his stereo and turned up the volume. The music covered the sound of a shotgun blast. Some time later, the stereo still playing loudly, his mother entered his room and turned on the light. He was dead, the shotgun still aimed at his heart.

Unhooked.

If only he had known there was another way.

THE TRAGEDY OF THE HOOKED

Laughing hysterically, Betty, a teen in a Midwestern town, ran downstairs in her home, grabbing lamps, vases, and pictures and smashing them against the wall. With almost superhuman strength, she knocked her mother to the floor. Then in a trance, she walked slowly and deliberately to the cage of her pet canary, opened the door, caught the bird, and ate it alive.

Betty then ran back upstairs and collapsed. Before medical help could be summoned, she lay lifeless on the floor.

It all started when Betty and a friend bought gum from a young man who claimed that his gum would help the girls chew their troubles away. An autopsy revealed Betty's psychotic behavior and death were the result of an overdose of LSD.

In Los Angeles two young men — one a star athlete — decided to play "chicken" one Saturday about midnight. They hopped into their cars and started at each other at breakneck speed. Both were determined not to be chicken. Suddenly there was a crash, the twisting of steel, a shattering of glass, and two bodies rolled unto the pavement. The two boys were taken to a Los Angeles hospital. One boy was dead on arrival, the other — the star athlete — is today paralyzed from his neck down.

Both boys, according to youth evangelist Frank Gonzales who often speaks to school assemblies on the evils of drugs, were high on marijuana.

Gonzales also tells the grisly story of the four youths who crossed the Mexican-California border and headed for Los Angeles with a load of heroin. That afternoon in Tijuana the four boys — all drug addicts — had decided that for them old-fashioned smuggling methods were out. Cleverly, they bought a bag of balloons and tied into each about an ounce of heroin. Then the four fellows each swallowed three balloons. Later at the border, they were searched and, of course, found clean.

But before they reached the San Diego city limits, one of the boys started reeling in the back seat. What had happened was obvious: one of the heroin-filled balloons had burst in his stomach. His three friends watched helplessly as the boy's face turned purple. Five minutes later the boy was dead.

The driver left the freeway and drove into the hills. There they dragged their friend's body out of the car, cut him open with switchblades, and pulled out the balloons. Then they stuck their fingers down their throats, gagged, and vomited up the other heroin-filled balloons.

These gruesome incidents are not unusual in the world of the hooked. They reflect a heinous malady that is afflicting young people of the now generation in epidemic proportions, from Maine to California and Florida to Washington and on into Canada, in cities large and small, in towns and hamlets. Increasingly, officialdom is beginning to act, but many adults, some of them parents, haven't comprehended the seriousness of the drug problem, and consider it

The Tragedy of the Hooked • 15

simply another youthful craze such as eating live goldfish or listening to rock 'n' roll music.

The drug culture, according to Vice-President Agnew, "threatens to sap our national strength unless we move hard and fast to bring it under control."

The consensus of a panel of experts addressing fourteen hundred physicians in New York City: If America does not solve its mushrooming drug addiction problem within the next ten years, "our civilization may find it difficult to survive."

In a speech given in July 1969, Dr. Hardin B. Jones, of Donner Laboratory, University of California, Berkeley, predicted, "If no remedy is found [to our drug problem], half of our young people may be so crippled or destroyed by drug abuse within the next three years that they may not be able to function as effective members of our society." Even if his statement proves only a fraction correct, the blight on youth cannot be shrugged off.

As evidence that even deaths attributed to drugs among young people are often accepted as routine news, the very week in May 1969 when all America and much of the Western world mourned the shooting of four Kent State students, seventeen young people, without much publicity, died in New York from overdoses of heroin. Since 1969, more than one thousand deaths from narcotics use have been recorded annually in New York.

Ironically, many youths who support the drug culture say they are using drugs to protest the Vietnam War; yet the numbers killed and maimed by drugs are probably much greater than those of the same ages killed or maimed in Vietnam in the same time period.

Berkeley's Dr. Jones goes to history for evidence of how a nation can be destroyed by drug abuse. "China," he says, "which prior to the nineteenth century, was one of the greatest civilizations on earth, was systematically destroyed by Western traders who brought opium into China under the pretense of medicinal purposes and then, when trade increased between China and the West, used opium as their major commodity in trade for China's tea, silk, and ceramics. By the beginning of the twentieth century, an estimated 29 percent of adult Chinese were opium addicts. Drugs in general are very close to destroying us. Of the 25 percent of all young people who now chronically use marijuana, half will be using heroin within a year and a half. Our peril is very great. This country has never had such a challenge."

When you consider the effect of drugs on the mind and body, the statements by Dr. Jones and others are better understood. Johnny Cash, the popular country and western singer, was hooked on drugs for seven years. A large man, six feet two inches, he normally weighed 240 pounds, but at the peak of his addiction he dropped to about 140 pounds. Lacking stamina and resistance, he often was too ill to appear for a performance. He became belligerent and short-tempered, and did such weird things as repainting a motel room to suit his taste and bringing a donkey and bales of hay into another room. Booking agents began to give up on him, until he miraculously kicked his habit in 1967 by will power from God, he testifies.

The Tragedy of the Hooked • 17

"Drugs rob your mind of love," he stated in an article in *Coronet* magazine. "You don't care about your friends or your loved ones, only about the drug. You get to hate the people who try to help you. In time, you lose your self-respect. You cease being a human being. You want to die, but you keep increasing your habit so you can live. Each increase puts you closer to death."

Those in the front lines of the fight against the drug problem cite heroin as the most deadly and the drug that most seriously affects American young people. Addiction usually means a short, torturous life; the user needs about thirty-five dollars a day to maintain his habit. Both sexes steal and rob, and women become prostitutes to buy heroin.

Obviously the pusher and the wholesaler get rich on their victims. On the street the price for a pound of heroin is $100,000, though it is worth only $2,500 a pound when it arrives in the U.S. (Eighty percent comes from the poppy fields of Turkey via Marseilles, France, where it is refined into heroin.)

Generally young people start with such drugs as marijuana or amphetamines (Methedrine, Desoxyn, Dexedrine, and Benzedrine) and move on to psychedelic drugs such as LSD, DMT, and STP. Far too many degenerate to heroin and other narcotics.

A lot of people who should know better argue for legalizing marijuana, saying it is safer than alcohol and that it is no more addictive than cigarettes. "There are more lies told and more misinformation given about marijuana . . . than about any other issue I know," asserts Dr. Hardin Jones. "Although marijuana does not lead to use of harder narcotics through *chemical* addiction, it promotes an attitude of curiosity about them and its use increases the chance of exposure to them."

It was at Berkeley that Timothy Leary initiated the age of the drug cult, and Dr. Jones has had opportunity to study users first hand. He says that many of those who at the outset began using drugs to "expand their perceptions" today "look aged and sick."

Eight physicians reported in late 1970 a newly discovered, sometimes fatal disease among users of dangerous drugs — especially methamphetamine, known to drug users as "speed" or "meth." About 10 percent of users will get the disease, one physician said. The disease destroys arteries leading to major organs — stomach, kidneys, small intestine, liver, pancreas — the report stated.

Christianity Today editor, Dr. Harold Lindsell, calls the drug problem "the greatest blot on today's youthful subculture" and challenges young people to consider the possibility that the current wave of drug abuse is being fomented by anti-American (and antihuman) interests. "Could they be pawns in an international intrigue that is proving more effective than nuclear blackmail and guerrilla warfare? This fact cannot be ignored: a cold-blooded enemy might well resort to such means," Lindsell says.

In his own words, acknowledged revolutionist Jerry Rubin, in his vile and filthy book, *Do It!*, boasts: "We've combined youth, music, sex, drugs, and rebellion with treason, and that's a combination hard to beat."

Mitchell Ware, head of the Illinois Bureau of Investigation, says hallucinogenic drugs have been present at every major campus demonstration in Illinois and that the drugs may have contributed to rioting.

For those who become wise to the curse of drugs, there is no simple way out — especially for those hooked on psychedelic drugs and narcotics.

Some are able to break the habit "cold turkey" — without the use of medication or medical care. But even these need help. Without doubt, programs offering spiritual aid have the highest percentage of cures. David Wilkerson's Teen Challenge Centers across the U.S. claim a 74 percent cure rate for addicts who receive Jesus Christ as Saviour and who cooperate for the full rehabilitation treatment. Many other Christian organizations conduct successful programs that result in addicts kicking the habit and living changed lives. (For a list of Christian organizations ministering to addicts, see the final pages of this book.) Local churches in many cities, as well as rescue missions, have also introduced addicts to Jesus Christ and He has given them power to become transformed people.

That's what this book is all about. The individual stories tell of addicts who in one way or another found their way to the Saviour and who today are living examples of His power to unhook the hooked!

JAMES R. ADAIR
Wheaton, Illinois

Note: In technical use, the words *addict*, *addiction*, and *hooked* relate to narcotics. However, in this book the terms are used in a broader sense. While certain non-narcotic drugs are not physically addictive, they are psychologically addictive. David Wilkerson says, for example, "I can tell you from firsthand experience that marijuana users become just as 'hooked' as persons addicted to heroin." J.R.A.

1. FROM OFF THE DESERT

by Miriam Schultz

I am a New Yorker and come from an Orthodox Jewish background. My parents are both Orthodox Jews and they sent me to a Hebrew school to study the Old Testament in depth. I learned much of the discipline and all of the laws that were involved and, so to speak, I was a very disciplined child.

When I was about twelve, I was very dissatisfied with my religion. It didn't give me the fulfillment I was looking for. I didn't mind a religion like that — you know, so easy — but I kept asking questions and getting no answers. I would try to pray when they told me to pray, but nothing seemed to work. I finally became rebellious and I was just very difficult to handle. Finally when I turned fifteen, a friend introduced me to amphetamines. Bennies, speed . . . they seemed so harmless and yet they could give you that "good feeling."

Later on, still only fifteen, I started smoking marijuana. This I thought was where it was at. I liked it, so I continued. I told myself I would never go on to anything more. But six months later, I took my first LSD trip. While high on LSD I looked up at the sky and realized that no matter who was with me, no matter to whom I belonged, I was nothing until I made things OK with whoever was upstairs and I looked up to the sky and said, "Oh, well, one of these days I'm going to know who You really are."

In 1968, when I was sixteen, I ran away from home and lived on the streets of New York. First I lived in a park, and when it got cold I went down into Greenwich Village. I walked the streets at night because I had no place to stay, no money; I couldn't work. I was high all the time.

Things were getting bad, and I couldn't go home. I knew that once I had left there was no going home. And my parents didn't send anyone after me, so I was on my own, trying to find out what life was all about. I finally got out to California, where I got deeply involved in drugs, and here I got to a point where I was dissatisfied. I was selling drugs; I was buying drugs. I had drugs all the time. But they didn't make me happy anymore. They were just another high. A friend of mine once said, "LSD is just an old movie. You see the same thing over and over again."

Well, I stopped using LSD. I came to New York again and I got involved in metaphysical meditation and all this type of religion — searching for God; searching for an answer to life, but there was none. No satisfaction. I would try one thing and it would last for a couple of days and I would be on to the next. I was constantly wandering. There was a time when I thought I was happy, but yet, how happy can a girl be when she keeps running? I had run from New York to California — back and forth, hitchhiking, looking for something, but never, never finding it.

From Off the Desert • 23

While in California I had met some Christians who told me about Christ. Being from an Orthodox Jewish family, I laughed: as far as I was concerned, Jesus Christ was just a religion, a church; these people were hung up. I didn't want anything to do with Jesus Christ. I was going to find out the truth. I wasn't going to follow someone else's philosophy or idea. I had to know the truth. I had come too far. I had taken too many drastic steps.

I became discouraged — I couldn't go home anymore, and drugs no longer did the trick. I finally went back to California and lived out in the desert. Metaphysical meditation didn't turn me on anymore. Buddhism wasn't the answer. So, I just sat there hoping for something to come along. One day a girl came out to the dessert to tell us about Jesus. I looked at her as if she was crazy and said, "Look, girl, I don't want to hear about no Jesus." I commented that I wanted to know the truth about life. She began to tell me how He was the Truth, and I scoffed. Finally she left.

But I was to see her again. Larry, the guy I was living with, became quite sick and begged me to get in touch with the girl who had talked about Jesus. Maybe she and her kind could pray and he would be healed. Emphatically, I told him if he wanted this girl and her crowd to pray for him, *he* could call or write her. I wasn't going to. I wanted nothing to do with this Jesus crowd — and for no conscious reason.

To my surprise, twelve days after my guy had written the letter to the Christians he was healed of hepatitis. We both knew that you don't get over hepatitis in twelve days. Larry told me that he was going to this Christian house to find out more about Jesus because Jesus had healed him. I told him he was crazy. I didn't know what to do. I didn't want to go. I didn't want to have anything to do with Jesus Christ. But somehow when he asked me to come along I said Yes.

When in March 1969 I came to this home in Anaheim, California — the home of Glen and Barbara Marshall — I was dirty. I was barefooted. My hair was straggly. My clothes were filthy. I had been hitchhiking on the road for days. And the first thing I sensed in that home was love. I had never in my life known love. I had always wanted it, but I never felt it as I felt it in this house. I didn't know what it was, but I wasn't going to let go of it so easily. At the house Barbara fed Larry and me and gave us a place to sleep — separately. She was stern, but she was loving, and even though she tried to discipline me from the very first, I took it because she did it in love.

The next day Barbara took us to church. It was the first time in my life I had ever been to a church, and it was a strange experience, so different from the synagogue of my childhood. At the end of the service (during which I laughed most of the way through), the pastor gave an altar call. It was an early morning service, and seeing everybody going up, I just went up. Somebody asked me if I wanted to be filled, and I said, "Filled? With what?"

He said, "With the Holy Spirit."

I said, "What's that?"

He said, "Well — Jesus."

And I said, "Jesus — who's he?"

He said, "Are you saved?"

I said, "Saved, what's that?" I just stood there; I didn't know what he was talking about.

Then a guy started telling me about Jesus and I just started giving him all these philosophies about Buddhism, Zen, Yoga, and where life was really at, really not believing it completely because I was not really satisfied in it. Well, nothing came of this conversation and Barbara took us home. I wanted to leave; I wanted just to get out of that place, but something kept me there. I wasn't going to let go of that love even though I wouldn't admit it.

Barbara made me listen to tapes. She made me realize what I was doing. She made me realize that there was a spiritual warfare going on and that when I speak to God I need to know Jesus in order to really know God. And I began to think, "Well, either Jesus Christ is real, or He isn't real. It's got to be one way or the other. There are no two ways about it." And I thought that if my search was sincere and was really for real, then I would look into this. I wouldn't let it pass me. A person truly searching will not live with a doubt, because you never know if you should have stopped then or not. So I said, "I'm going to find out if Jesus is real. If He's real I've got to do something about it. If He's not real, I just want to get it out of my mind and never have to think about it again. So then when someone approaches me about it, I can just turn them off because I know. But first I've got to find out."

That night we went back to church. This time I went with a completely different feeling. This time I was going to find out the truth. Before I went into the church, something just kept tugging at my

26 • UNHOOKED

heart and I just couldn't go in. I wanted to, but I couldn't. I finally walked out into the parking lot, and I began to cry. I cried all the tears of loneliness, all the tears of misery that I had kept inside since I had left home. I was a miserable little girl and I didn't know where to turn.

I finally raised my hands up to the sky, and I cried, "God, the Father of Abraham, Isaac and Jacob — I know about You. I studied about You in school and I know You are real, but what about this guy Jesus? Is He really Your Son? Is He really real? God, if Jesus is Your Son, You know about Him, and if You know about Him, You can tell me about Him. God, if You tell me about Jesus, I will follow Him. I want to do what is right, but I don't know." I continued, "God, I'm a Jew, and I need a sign tonight. I can't wait any longer. I can't live with a doubt in my heart. Please show me."

When I walked into the church I didn't hear one word of the sermon. I didn't understand what was going on. It was a big church and at the end of the service, the pastor gave an altar call. I didn't even know what an altar was, but something in my heart kept saying, "Go up front. Go up to the front of the church." And I thought, "That's silly. I can't get out my seat. People will look at me — dirty, ragged, and they will laugh at me." But something inside said, "What do you care what people have to say? You've gone through too much. You've come too far to have to worry about them." And I thought, "Wow, what should I do?"

And about that time everybody was standing and singing the closing hymn and I didn't see anybody up at the front of the church because I was so far

From Off the Desert • 27

back. But I knew that that was where I belonged. And right before the church service ended, I couldn't hold back anymore. I ran up there. I got up to the altar, and I saw all of those people standing in line up there, and I just thought, "What are all of those people doing up there?" And I got in line with them and as soon as I got in line with them the pastor lifted up his head as though God had just spoken to him and said, "She just came home." He looked at me and he started to cry, and he said, "Praise the Lord." Well, the first thing that came out of my mouth was, "Praise the Lord."

Suddenly God spoke to my heart and He said, "Jesus is real. He is My Son. You follow Him from this day on and He'll never lead you wrong." God said to me, "There's a lot of things you won't understand at first, but trust in Him. Hold on to Him. Believe in His name and He'll see you through and He'll explain these things to you slowly." I knew I had come home. This great peace, this great joy just filled my soul like I had never known before.

It was at this moment that I understood the love that was in Barbara's home. I realized that it was God's love that had captured my heart and I gave my life to Jesus Christ and I told Him, "Lord Jesus, I am a nobody, I'm nothing; I am miserable. Please change my life and help me."

I knew I was saved. I knew that my life had been transformed that very moment because I knew I had finally come home. I had met God at His fullest. I had met God through Jesus Christ. The Scripture, "I am the Way, the Truth and the Life; no man cometh unto the Father but by Me," became so real to me because I had spent so much of my

28 • UNHOOKED

life searching for God. I knew there was a God, but I couldn't find Him. But the day I met Jesus Christ I met the true and living God.

The pastor took those of us who had come forward into another room to pray with us. And he hit me with the question, "Do you want to be filled with the Holy Spirit?" Well, I kinda chuckled and said, "What's that? I don't know anything about that." Somebody said, "It's power from on high. God wants to fill you with His Holy Spirit that you can bear witness and He will give you strength in the Christian walk." And I felt my face still glowing and a big smile cross my face from the experience I had just had. I said, "Look, God has just showed me that Jesus was His Son. If this Holy Spirit is from God, and if He wants me to have it, what do you have to do to get it?" He said, "All you have to do is to ask God and He'll give Him to you."

I raised my hands, and they laid hands on me, and I said, "God, if it is from You and if it will help me, please give it to me now." And the greatest love and joy just began to fill my soul. I was content for the first time in my life. I had stopped running. I was finally home.

Barbara and Glen Marshall took Larry (who also trusted Christ) and me home with them, and they kept me for two months. I lived with them, and I started reading the Bible. I thought the New Testament was like the Old Testament, but I soon found it to be different. Jesus Christ became real to me. He became my all in all.

I came back to New York to share my experience with my parents and they were really upset because they couldn't understand. I was kind of lost and hopeless, but I knew Jesus would see me through. And then I met the Rev. John Benton and he told me about The Walter Hoving Home, the Teen Challenge home for girls in Garrison, New York. I asked him if I could come up to the Home and he accepted me into the program.

I have completed the program at the girls' home (one year in length). As I write this, I am entering Bible school at Teen Challenge Institute of Missions in Rhinebeck, New York. It's been more than a year since I've known Jesus Christ, and I know He is the only real answer to life because He is the only answer to my life. I tried all there was to try and I was still just as miserable. I did it and it was done . . . there was no lasting effect. When Jesus came into my life He taught me what life was all about. He picked me off the desert of life and filled me when I was dissatisfied, and He gave me life that I wouldn't trade for anything in the world. And I thank Jesus Christ for being so real. I thank Him for dying on the cross, for shedding His blood for me, for making me — a sinner — realize that I needed help, for showing me that the only way to get to God is through Him.

2. COUGH SYRUP: MY DOWNFALL

by John Morgan as told to James R. Adair

When I went from junior high to high school I began a real search for what was going on. I really wanted to know what was happening.

To begin with, I had been turned off by some church people who had double standards — people who preached one thing and lived another. I had made professions of faith in Christ on a couple of occasions. But I decided all of this wasn't for me.

In time I began going with some guys looking for trouble — like driving around to drive-ins and drinking beer and beating people up. Then in a rough section of Charlotte, North Carolina, my home town, I got beat up pretty badly. I thought I was a big man. I wasn't.

In the eleventh grade I got into the hip set. "A lot of being hip is doing drugs," my friends said. I was scared stiff of marijuana — I'd always heard, "Don't mess with it," and I had decided not to.

One of my friends had another angle. "Look, you don't have to smoke marijuana; man, you can get just as stoned on cough syrup. Drink a whole bottle of this stuff and you're out of your mind. It's fabulous!"

And he was right. You do. I must have gotten

Cough Syrup: My Downfall • 31

stoned thirty or forty times on cough syrup. I was, I guess, a cough syrup freak. Later I read the label and discovered that the stuff had chloroform and alcohol in it; I figured that was making me stoned. So I decided not to mess with it anymore.

I started smoking marijuana after that and took speed for about a year. At this point I had reached a state of mind where I just didn't care about anything. Some people peddle the idea that marijuana doesn't really lessen a person's ability to make reasonable and responsible decisions. Well, I can vouch that it does. It does lessen a person's ability to think. And I know this, too — it lessens your ability to resist other drugs. In the atmosphere where marijuana is smoked, all other drugs are available — LSD and all the rest.

In February 1969 I started taking LSD. I took it with a girl friend who urged me to try it. My first trip I didn't like; the second one I really liked.

I managed to hide my drug play from my parents. I'd come home and say, "I don't feel good. Got a headache. I'm going to my room." I'd turn on my record player and live in my own little world.

Finally in the summer of '69 my parents caught on. I looked the part of a real hippie — long hair and typical hip dress. Physically, my body was in bad shape, and my mind too.

After a while LSD affects your mind to the point where you become schizophrenic — you're one person and then another. You become paranoid — you're always scared you're going to get busted. You're scared of people that you do drugs with — maybe they're informers, and you get really shaky.

32 • UNHOOKED

My folks caught on, and my father couldn't take me any longer and "invited" me to leave. I went to live with a friend.

Once I took some bad LSD and got strychnine poisoning. They use strychnine as a catalyst to hurry the process of making LSD, and sometimes in these bathroom labs some poison gets in with the LSD. I got violently ill. But it didn't hold me down; I still wanted to do drugs. Somehow maybe I'd reach God by getting high on drugs. But that's really a lie; nobody ever really reached God on drugs.

Meantime, I went to summer school and worked. When payday came I knew exactly who to take my paycheck to in order to get my drugs. I pushed drugs, selling to other kids. The supplier I got my drugs from would sell me three or four hundred LSD tabs for two dollars and I'd sell them for as much as five dollars. At that time a drug ring was bringing in maybe one or two thousand tabs at one time into Charlotte.

The LSD trip I remember best happened at the house when my buddy Phil was living with a married couple. A friend of ours came in. He was in this drug ring. He handed me a tablet of LSD and said, "Here try this; it's only two days old. Good stuff — just flown in from Los Angeles." It usually takes up to thirty days to get LSD to the low man on the totem pole. And the fresher it is, the more potent it is.

I crunched up the tablet into a fine powder and snorted it up my nose. About ten minutes later I was tripping so heavily that I had to sit down. You've heard of wall hallucinations? Instead of

Cough Syrup: My Downfall • 33

just one wall, I had one, two, three, four walls of hallucinations. Snarling, growling faces came out of the walls, the floor, the ceiling. They were eating at my flesh, eating at my soul, at my total being. I was completely freaked out — a candidate for jumping out a window or shooting myself.

Next thing I knew I had reached over and picked up a Bible from the coffee table next to my chair. "God," I said, "is this going to let me down too?" Just why I said it, I don't know; up to this point I didn't want anything to do with God because of my experience with church people.

I hugged it to me. When you are on LSD sometimes you hang on to things for security — a rock, a flower. I held on to that Bible. I felt warm inside. I walked outside, trying to gather my thoughts. I came back inside, and my friend Phil, who in recent weeks had started a comeback through Jesus, began talking to me.

"God has a plan and purpose for you that only you can fulfill," he said. He told me that Jesus Christ died on a cross for my sins and came alive from the grave. "The love and power that brought the Son of God from the grave is also the love and power that can save your soul from an eternal hell."

This is what I had been searching for — I wanted to know the truth. I wanted to know exactly what was going on.

Remember the woman in the Bible who had the issue of blood and reached out and grabbed Christ's garment? She was completely healed. At this last moment as I was going down, I just reached out. I asked God to just help me, to heal me.

But I made a mistake. I tried to bargain with

God. I was saying, "I'll do drugs some and still believe in Jesus too!" I did not have the power to quit drugs — or other sins I was involved in.

Then right after Thanksgiving I sought God in a deeper way. I gave myself completely to the Holy Spirit. Jesus had saved me; now His Spirit was beginning to have all of me. Till then I was being pulled back to the old life. In the power of the Holy Spirit I gave up drugs completely.

God has led me to a sound church and He has given me the power to get up in front of people and give my testimony. He has helped me understand the Scriptures better. I have a new love for people — my parents, for example. I'm back living with them. Don't get me wrong — I still have problems. Once, I remember, Mom asked me to mow our lawn (two and a half acres of grass). I didn't do it; then the Holy Spirit spoke to me, and I ended up calling her on the phone to ask her forgiveness and to say I'd be home to get the job done. I remember also telling my dad that I loved him, and our relationship changed after that.

I told my mom I was even willing to cut my hair for her. It's just hair, you know. If the Lord wants me to cut my hair for them — if I can make their life a little bit happier, I want to do that. Jesus was a servant. He even washed people's feet.

I've learned to go to the Lord with all my problems. I needed a new motorcycle. "Lord, I got this old motorcycle here," I told Him. "If You want me to have a better one, please work out something so I can keep up the payments." You know, the guy I went to about a trade didn't even look at my old motorcycle. He just said, "OK, $250

Cough Syrup: My Downfall • 35

and your old one." It was what I could afford, but I hadn't dreamed that I could get that kind of a deal.

This new bike has plenty of power — but the power I like is the new power God has given me. I am going to stand firm on Christ. I'm going to stay with Jesus.

Not long after he told his story, John Morgan was inducted into the Army. While stationed at Fort Sam Houston in Texas, he suffered a severe attack of spinal meningitis. His parents were called and informed that there was little hope of his surviving. His mother put out an SOS to John's friends to pray for him. With many calling on God to spare John, his fever broke the next day, John reports, and a few days later he had recovered. He was home on a thirty-day leave when he gave this report and checked the facts in his story just prior to publication.

3. SUICIDE WAS MY SOLUTION

by Domingo Garcia
as told to Muriel Larson

I was on my way to the top of the building to commit suicide. I'd just jump off and my miserable existence would be ended! I was twenty-one years old and had been enslaved by drugs for more than seven years. Whenever I wasn't under the influence of drugs the torturing memories came back to me — as they did now. . . .

My mother's face came before me. Not the face she had had when I was a little boy in Puerto Rico. No, her toothless, smashed, bleeding face as it had been after my drunken father had gotten through beating her unconscious before my very eyes! Plastic surgery had helped somewhat — but my father continued to beat my mother whenever he got drunk, which was often.

We had moved to the United States in the hope that a new environment might help my dad stop drinking. Not only did that hope fail, however, but the move proved to be a bad one for my brother Eddie and me.

When I was fourteen years old and living in Brooklyn, New York, I was approached by a boy named Frankie, the president of the Roman Lords. "How about joining our gang?" he asked me.

"What do I have to do?" I wondered.

"Oh, we have initiation rites, of course," he said. That was an understatement. The five leaders of the gang took turns beating, punching, and kicking me until, bruised and bleeding, I fell unconscious. But because I didn't cry out in pain the whole time, I was in.

A few months later they tested me to see if I were trustworthy. "See that fellow coming down the street?" one of my friends said. "Well, he's a member of the Hellburners [a rival gang]. Go up to him and stick your blade in his stomach. That way we'll know you're not chicken."

I had a sick feeling inside. But I had to prove myself. I walked up to the fellow and asked, "What gang are you a member of?"

I could see him reaching for his blade as he answered. He said grimly, "Hellburners!" Then we went at each other. I felt my blade cutting into his stomach . . . and he fell to the sidewalk! There were no witnesses other than my gang friends. We got out of there fast. But the memory of the stricken boy pursued me and gave me no peace.

"Here, Dom, what you need is some marijuana," one of the members of my gang said. He handed me a stick of it. "This'll make you forget what you did today." But though it blurred my mind, I couldn't forget. *The stabbing, the stabbing,* my heart kept crying.

Later an older man came in. "Here, kid," he said, "I've got something stronger than marijuana." He took me into another room and produced a hypodermic needle. As he prepared some heroin he said, "This is the greatest shot you'll ever have in your life . . . the greatest thrill. All your problems will be forgotten!"

I'll forget the stabbing, I thought, *and my drunken father and my poor beaten mother. . . .* The man came at me with the hypo, and for a moment I held back from him. Then he slammed it into my arm. My mind started to go up into the clouds . . . my problems dropped away.

I heard him laughing. "Why are you laughing?" I asked foggily.

He took out a small package. "Because from now on every time you need a shot of narcotics, it will cost you five dollars," he answered.

It broke my mother's heart when she accidentally found out one day that I was an addict. "Domingo, my son," she cried, "what are you doing? You're destroying your life!" But she couldn't help me. And I couldn't help myself.

When my brother Eddie learned that I was shooting drugs, he tried them himself. Soon he was an addict and started mugging, shoplifting, and stealing to support his habit. One evening both of us were desperate for some drugs. Eddie was like a wild man. He grabbed a young man and threw him to the sidewalk. "Get his money," he told me. I did.

We went and bought sixty dollars' worth of narcotics and used them all that night. We forgot what we had done. Toward morning we walked back on the same street. The young man we had robbed came running toward us demanding his money back. "Eddie, watch out!" I cried. "He has a blade in his hand!" But before he could defend himself, Eddie's face was slit through from his left ear to

Suicide Was My Solution • 39

his mouth. I could see his teeth through the deep slit!

We hailed a passing car which took us to the hospital. When Eddie came out two hours later, he had thirty-six stitches in his face. We went home. My mother touched his face lightly . . . and fainted.

My father and sister came in and tried to revive her. They saw Eddie's face and he quickly told what had happened. They were on their knees beside my mother. They looked up at me, pointed their fingers, and cried, "You're to blame for this. You got Eddie on narcotics!"

I was disgusted with myself. My whole family had turned against me. As I started to walk out, however, my mother came to and gave me sort of a pleading look, as if to say, "Come back, my son." But fear of my father kept her from saying anything. I left home that day.

After that I forgot about everybody. I stole anything I could get my hands on to support my habit. I was in and out of jail. At the age of twenty-one I was jailed again — and my old gang friend and fellow addict, Frankie, was in the next cell.

He had just shot a man who had caught him burglarizing his apartment.

"I can't take it any more, Domingo!" he cried out to me. He made a rope out of his sheet. Before the guard came in answer to my cries, Frankie had hung himself before my very eyes.

The next day I was released from jail. And that was when I decided I couldn't take it any more either. Yes, I was going up to the top of the building to commit suicide.

But a man was on his way down those stairs.

And he stopped me. "Say, I've seen you before," he said. "You're a drug addict, aren't you? Well, I don't know what you're about to do — but young man, no matter what you've done, Jesus loves you!"

"You mean somebody loves me?" I asked, astonished.

"Young man, Jesus loves you," he said again. Imagine Jesus loving me, a filthy, lousy drug addict! The man gave me a card. It said, "Teen Challenge Training Center." He put his arm around me. Somebody cared for me! He took me downstairs and pointed me in the direction of the Center . . . and made sure I went.

When I got there, someone met me at the door and took me into the chapel. Several boys came too and they all talked to me about the Lord and how He could help me. I told them about my problems. "There's no hope for me," I said despairingly. I started out the door. But Nicky Cruz was standing in the way.

"Domingo, come, let's pray for you," he said.

There on my knees all the agony of my life flashed before me. I was filled with pain. They told me about Christ dying on the cross for my sins and I thought about it. I cried out, "O God, forgive me. Save me, Jesus, save me!" I felt the lovingkindness of God coming into my life. The pain was gone! At that very moment I was healed of my addiction. Jesus did a miracle for me! Suicide had been my solution but a new life was God's solution.

After that I became burdened for other young people who were enslaved by drugs. The Lord led me to Toccoa Falls Bible College in Georgia in 1965.

Suicide Was My Solution • 41

While I was a student there, my still-addicted brother came down by train. My mother phoned me and cried, "I can't do a thing with him, Domingo. He's stealing everything in the house to buy drugs. I've sent him down to you!"

The president of the school kindly allowed Eddie to stay as a visitor. Eddie came off drugs cold turkey and was very sick for a while. But he enjoyed the atmosphere of the school. And he committed his life to Christ. Now he is happily married to a lovely Christian girl. (And so am I.) My mother, father, sister, and a number of other relatives have also been saved. I have been off drugs now for six years.

The Lord has opened the way for me to start the Youth Challenge Training Center of Greater Greenville, South Carolina, which opened in May 1970. I was concerned for the South, since I had found that there was no such place to help rehabilitate addicts there. We now have a large building with thirty-five rooms in Travelers Rest, north of Greenville.

We keep fellows here for six months and instruct them in the Bible and fundamentals of the Christian faith. The Lord has given us a vision concerning this work, and we hope to start a similar home for girl addicts, as well as a farm.

My favorite Bible verse is I Corinthians 1:27 — "But God hath chosen the foolish things of the world to confound the wise; and God hath chosen the weak things of the world to confound the things which are mighty."

4. I WAS THE PUSHERS' PLAYTHING

by Paddy Duncan*
as told to Monte C. Unger

I had the eerie feeling I was being watched, but I knew I was all alone because I had entered the empty shopping arcade in London by myself.

"Alone at last," I thought. How enjoyable not to have to talk to anyone. I had had a busy day at work and just wanted quiet.

Naturally I was slightly annoyed when the arcade began filling with people. Some jostled against me. I turned to glance at the strangers, the way you do when someone in a crowd presses against you, making you feel uncomfortable.

Fear gripped me. I knew them all. All old friends — but they weren't smiling. They were tight-lipped. Grim. So I *had* been followed!

They were members of my old gang in Soho, London's notorious nightclub district, where I used to play the piano to pay for the heroin I needed.

But that was all behind me. I had met some wonderful new friends who had helped me kick the heroin habit (I was mainlining — shooting heroin directly into the veins, the worst form of nar-

---

*Her surname has been changed at Paddy's request. Paddy lives in London, England.

I Was the Pushers' Playthting • 43

cotics addiction). These new friends had allowed me to stay at their flat and accepted me as a person. And eventually they had even introduced me to a personal relationship with Jesus Christ.

I had come a long way for a girl who was ready to die two years earlier at age twenty-two.

At least I thought the old life was all behind me. But one of the gang knocked me to the pavement. The others surrounded me so passers-by wouldn't see the scuffle. They kicked and beat me.

Then came the worst part. Someone rolled up my sleeve and held my arm tightly. My vein bulged, a smooth dark blue ridge running down my arm. He shoved a hypodermic needle into the vein. I was a heroin addict again!

Someone kicked me hard in the ribs and they left. Now I really was alone!

The gang was jealous of me. Jealous of my new clean world. And probably afraid I would tell the police of their criminal activities.

Now what would my new friends say? These girls who had stayed up with me night after night helping me through the awful withdrawal pains?

Would they help me even again? Or would they think the beating was contrived so I could have another go at the short-lived delights of heroin? Would this be the end of my new life?

These were my thoughts while riding the train back to the flat.

How did I get started in the life-destroying world of narcotics in the first place?

At a London party when I was sixteen a friend offered me a "reefer" or "hash," two of the many names for marijuana in England.

I didn't particularly want to smoke a reefer, but I didn't want to stand out, either. I was the youngest person there and everyone else was smoking them.

My first reefer made me sick.

But because of crowd pressure, I smoked another. Then another. The third one was slightly uplifting, but still nothing terribly exciting.

Then came the pills. Someone said they were easier to take than marijuana. And they were easy to hide.

Age seventeen, and I was hooked on pills.

Something happened at school that made me realize, for the first time since I'd started drugs, the seriousness of it all. In preparation for a difficult exam I took some pills. We called them "bennies," for Benzedrine. They kept me awake and alert during the long test. I felt absolutely wonderful. I thought I had answered all the questions correctly and written reams and reams of answers.

The following day the headmistress asked to see me. She handed me yesterday's exam. I was horrified. I had written the same sentence over and over again for three hours. I didn't remember doing that. I'd thought the exam was so easy.

However, I took pills for three more years.

Then came the greatest delusion of all: heroin. I was twenty. I don't know really what started me. I do know that I didn't get the same effect with pills as before. And I was especially depressed during those days.

I felt *I* wouldn't get hooked on heroin. Not me. Another friend (I realized later that these weren't really "friends" at all) said that one shot of heroin

I Was the Pushers' Playthinq • 45

would be cheaper and quicker than pills. So I started "skin-popping." This is just lifting up the skin slightly and injecting heroin beneath the surface.

But narcotics is a gnawing monster that is *never* fully satisfied. Smoking marijuana wasn't enough. Pills weren't enough. And heroin under the skin wasn't enough.

I soon started mainlining. This is the moment the whole hoodlum world of narcotics pushers and suppliers waits for. I now became their plaything. People use you. Prices go up. You need the stuff so much that you even rob for it.

But it wasn't until after a big robbery caper that I realized I was getting involved in something that could destroy me. One night our gang broke into a shop. The owners, an old man and his wife, lived upstairs. They came down when they heard us banging around. The gang mercilessly beat them up while I watched.

Though I was on heroin at the time, this really shocked me. I had never been so close to physical violence before. Then I began wondering if I could ever stop drugs if I tried. It dawned on me that I couldn't. I was hooked. This was it. I became desperate.

So I took the first positive steps to get off drugs. I withdrew medically. But soon I went back to heroin. I tried again, but went back. I tried cold turkey, then soon went back. I was in a slippery cage and couldn't get out. I realized the end would soon be death. At age twenty-two I decided to take an overdose and get it all over with. It didn't work. Taken to a hospital, I recovered.

Even after this I went back to mainlining.

About this time I began rooming with a girl who worked with me. She had strange friends, I thought. They were happy, played the guitar, and sang Christian songs. I thought they were all quite odd. Then one night, one of the girls began talking to me about Jesus Christ. Just like that. It embarrassed me. I'd been to church only once or twice in my life. I never thought about God or Jesus or the Bible. But this person Jesus Christ was so real to this girl that I listened.

This girl, Judy, left England to live in New Zealand. But before she left we had become good friends and I heard lots more about Jesus, though I still never would do anything about it.

By letter, Judy suggested I visit another London girl named Pat Lawler, who is responsible for The Navigators (an international interdenominational Christian service organization) ministry among young women in the London area.

I didn't know if I should visit Pat or not. I kept thinking that if I were her, *I wouldn't have anything to do with the likes of me.* But out of desperation I called her. I was so afraid in those days.

Pat also talked to me about Christ. I still refused to get involved with God, but did withdraw again at another institution. Just as quickly I went back on drugs.

Pat told me I could get off drugs permanently — through Christ. I didn't see the connection between Christ and my dilemma. But I wanted to break the habit so much that I withdrew by the cold turkey method right in Pat's living room. The Navigator girls stayed with me constantly for three days,

I Was the Pushers' Playthink • 47

comforting me as I suffered the agonizing pains.

Withdrawal from heroin mainlining is terrible. You have tight, knife-sharp cramps in your stomach and in most of your muscles. You vomit. You sweat. You have hallucinations. And the worst part is the cramps in your throat. You can't breathe and you're sure you will die.

But at the end of three days, I had withdrawn. And I had learned that these girls were true friends. Pat let me move into her flat. It was a new start in life, though as yet I had no interaction with God.

After a few days, I returned to my job. On my first day back I began suffering acute withdrawal pains (an addict's body is so accustomed to drugs that these cramps occur for several months after withdrawal).

Soho was only ten minutes away. I was in agony, so I called someone who could bring me a shot. But while waiting for the contact to come to the phone, I thought again about what Pat had said about God. Had I really given Him a chance? I'd tried everything else and all had failed. In a few minutes I would be back in the middle of this nightmare.

So I hung up before the pusher answered. I prayed. I asked Christ to take charge of my life and to help me overcome drugs.

It seems miraculous, I know, but just after I prayed, the withdrawal cramps left. I simply couldn't believe it at the time. I'd withdrawn many times before, but nothing like this had ever happened.

I told the girls that night what I had done. They were elated. Later that evening the cramps did come back, as they would many times in the next six months. But God had not let me down on that first test of faith.

The girls suggested that I memorize I Corinthians 10:13 and quote the verse each time the cramps returned. The verse says, "No temptation has overtaken you that is not common to man. God is faithful, and He will not let you be tempted beyond your strength, but with the temptation will also provide the way to escape, that you may be able to endure it."

And it worked.

I never again had to take heroin. I was no longer an addict.

I began studying the Bible regularly, replacing old ugly thoughts with new life-changing concepts.

I'd made all this progress, then that disastrous day with the gang in the arcade . . . the beating . . . the heroin injection . . . the lonely train ride back to the flat as I wondered if my new life had come to a screeching end.

I left the train and limped to the apartment.

Pat saw my anguish, the caked blood, and the heroin's effect. She looked me right in the eyes.

I glanced away from her questioning face, then looked right back again for *I had to know what Pat was thinking.* Would she turn me away?

The answer came. Pat smiled, put her arm around me, and said, "Lie down here. Let's get you all cleaned up and back together again."

A friend that smiled.

I joyfully wept.

I stayed on with Pat. The rib that had been broken in the arcade battle healed. The severe withdrawal pains from the recent heroin shot came and

I Was the Pushers' Playthink • 49

went. The new life continued.

But there were other beatings. Other forced injections. Other ghosts of the past to be dealt with.

Finally the gang began to dissolve. Most died of narcotics. One or two just disappeared. And one other also became a Christian.

Now I am a student at a teacher training college and am leading a Navigators ministry on that campus.

During 1969 I held informal "coffee" evenings and Bible studies in my flat. By the end of the year twenty-two young women had surrendered their lives to Christ.

One girl, named Alison, was invited to do some investigative Bible studies. During the second lesson she was so unresponsive that I began relating the story of how I had overcome heroin with God's help.

Alison became very attentive. When she went back to her room that night she could only think of my story. She couldn't go to sleep. She knew what she must do. She asked Christ to come into her life that night.

There *are* miracles in the twentieth century. This is one. I seemed to be beyond hope, yet now I am helping other girls get right with God. The pushers' plaything has become Christ's free woman.

5. DISC JOCKEY ON A NEW TRIP

by James R. Adair

The time: an afternoon in August 1965. The setting: Shea Stadium, New York City. The Mets are out of town and the Beatles are the attraction. Sixty thousand screaming members of the hip generation suddenly become quiet as a drummer begins beating out a crashing, frenzied rhythm. Onto the platform on the field walks a long-haired young man in mod clothes: Nehru jacket, boots, and all.

He's Scott Ross, popular young man about town, an ex-disc jockey on WBIC, Bay Shore, Long Island, New York, who is about to introduce the Beatles.

Scott is an old hand at it, having traveled with and emceed for the Rolling Stones, the Animals, and other top rock groups.

The crowd applauds wildly, and Scott stands nonchalantly waiting, waving, smiling. When you've been around you get used to applause — but you always like it.

That was yesterday. Scott Ross no longer emcees for hit groups around the New York area, nor elsewhere for that matter.

He's back on radio, though, with "The Scott Ross Show" and is currently on more than thirty stations

Disc Jockey on a New Trip • 51

— some for two hours at a crack. Though he plays rock tunes for pop music lovers, there's something radically different about Scott. He doesn't yak about trivialities throughout the program; he talks good sense and, in comments and interviews, seeks to acquaint listeners with his new Friend, Jesus Christ.

He's been turned on by Jesus, Scott says. Not only has he found forgiveness of sin through the Saviour but he has a brand new life. He often travels with a group of young people known as The Newine and tells school crowds and others that one mark of the change is the freedom that has become his. And one particular freedom he enjoys is to be no longer hung up on dope.

And therein lies a story of near tragedy and comeback.

In his years in New York radio, first with WINS (as assistant music director) and then for a short hitch on WBIC as a deejay specializing in picking new hits and interviewing rock personalities, Scott made many friends in the pop music world. And he knew them all, it seemed — the Dave Clarke Five; Peter, Paul, and Mary; the Rascals; the Animals; and the Rolling Stones (not to mention the Beatles). He once commented that all of the rock personalities he knew were on "a big search for truth."

It was such a search for truth that took twenty-eight-year-old Scott Ross into the Maharesi's Eastern philosophies and down the drug trail — using ups (amphetamines), then marijuana, and finally LSD. At one point along the trail he was busted for possession.

It was on the summer night of the famous New York electrical power blackout in 1965 that Scott

52 • UNHOOKED

first tried marijuana. With a group of friends, he joined in smoking pot, for there seemed to be nothing much else to do in the dark.

"After that I smoked grass all the time," Scott says. By this time he was out of radio and writing for *Night Owl,* a trade publication in the entertainment field.

Because of his excellent background, one might conclude that Scott shouldn't have been so far off course in his quest for truth and happiness. Scott's father was a preacher who for many years opened a well-worn Bible and proclaimed Christ as the Way, the Truth, and the Life. He did so until his death about 1960. But somewhere Scott had turned off after the family had moved from Scotland to the United States in 1949.

When Scott Ross' mother discovered her talented son had become a drug user, she heartbrokenly prayed more than ever for him to open his life to God. When he visited her at her home in Hagerstown, Maryland, he sometimes flaunted his marijuana habit, and the little Scottish woman went to her room and got on her hotline to heaven. She believed with all her heart that "the effectual fervent prayer of a righteous [wo]man availeth much" (James 5:16).

Scott's experience with ups and marijuana set him up for a more potent drug. On New Year's Day 1966 on Broadway in New York City he met a friend, a schoolteacher, and they rapped for a while. Scott told him of his futile quest for truth, of his basic dissatisfaction with life. That gnawing something inside wouldn't be satisfied.

A look of concern swept the friend's face. "I've

Disc Jockey on a New Trip • 53

got something that will give you an answer to a lot of things," the man said, as if he had found the key to life.

The pair drove to New Jersey, where the teacher introduced Scott to Timothy Leary's way of life — lysergic acid diethylamide, better known as LSD.

"After that I became a real tripper," Scott says.

There were times he thought he was reaching new truths as psychedelic trips seemed to usher him into mysterious spiritual realms. But more and more the trips led him to the brink of insanity. Walls appeared to move; colors seemed stronger and more brilliant. Unusual patterns unfolded seemingly before his eyes. There were days he felt extremely depressed; and during other periods he seemed happy and sad at the same time.

Then came unusually bad trips. Once he became convinced that he was Adolf Hitler. On his last — and most mind-twisting — trip he thought he was Jesus Christ.

This hellish trip started when he took fifteen hundred micrograms of acid, six times the usual dosage. "Things got crazy," he recalls, wincing and saying that it hurts to think about it now. "Walls melted away, chains banged against the door. I didn't come down from that flight to the far reaches of my mind for six months!"

During the period he lost all control of his bodily functions and had hallucinations off and on for weeks and weeks. He tried to commit suicide several times.

Then for three months he thought he was Jesus Christ. "At times, I was even searching my hands and wrists for the nail holes," he remembers.

54 • UNHOOKED

While in the grip of the drug, Scott Ross prayed for help. Somewhere out there he hoped the God of his parents would hear. At the time of his trip, he shared an apartment with members of the Rolling Stones. Other groups dropped by frequently.

"Our apartment was the place to be," he says. "We practically had LSD flowing from the faucets."

Finally, a whipped, confused young man, he began praying one winter day in 1966 in Central Park. As pigeons fluttered about looking for a handout, bits of the Gospel message filtered through his mind. Jesus, he had heard his parents say, could come into a person's life and change things completely; He could enable a man to lick a habit, even to kick drugs.

"Jesus, if You're real like they say You are, please come into my life," the voice known to NYC rock fans whispered toward heaven.

After that, his life began to take on new meaning and new direction. Good things began happening. No longer was he happy with drugs, and he never went back to them.

Scott Ross says he has found the answer to his quest for truth. "That answer," he declares, "is Jesus Christ." He flatly discredits LSD as aiding in his quest for answers. "I did not find Jesus Christ through LSD," he says emphatically.

Ross quips that the Bible is the greatest trip he's ever taken. He says those who will believe in the Christ of the Bible and give Him control of their lives will experience a trip that is out of sight — LSD trips are totally inferior in comparison. He enjoys pointing out thrilling trips taken by Bible characters. "God talked John up into a trip that no

Disc Jockey on a New Trip • 55

one has figured out yet when He showed Him the wonders and terrors yet to come," Scott says, referring to the Book of The Revelation.

Young people naturally go for Scott in a big way. He still leans toward mod clothing, wears his hair moderately long, and continues to talk like a deejay. At one youth rally he quipped, "I have trouble getting up and saying things like 'amen' and 'hallelujah,' so I just say 'groovy.' "

Ross hits hard at drugs. To him LSD is "Lucifer's Satanic Drug." At a Methodist conclave of sixty-three hundred people in Richmond, in 1970, Virginia Governor Linwood Holton got Scott's message loud and clear. The governor mentioned in his address that marijuana is not addictive. Scott reminded the audience, when it came his turn, that while pot is not physically addictive, it is mentally addictive. Afterward, the governor sent an aide to talk with Scott about some of his views on the drug problem.

When Scott Ross and his Newine group invade high schools and other places, God's power comes into sharp focus. In Canton, Ohio, several hundred young people, many of them on drugs, came backstage in a high school auditorium to receive spiritual counsel, many committing their lives to Jesus for the first time. In Roanoke and Martinsville, Virginia, doors opened wide as Ross and company moved in with their message of spiritual liberation. The YMCA was jammed two nights in a row. The entire cheerleading squad at a high school professed Christ as Saviour, and scores of students dumped their drugs down bathroom drains.

On the other side of the coin, Scott and Newine

have run head-on into hatred for their message. At a college a hostile crowd surrounded the group — "until the Lord softened their hearts and we prayed with many as they accepted Jesus into their lives," Scott recounts. In Brooklyn a few weeks later they sang as young people on drugs began breaking up furniture. Here a boy with a knife threatened Bob Wyley, a Newiner. "In the boldness of the Lord, Bob stood his ground and twenty-five minutes later led the knife wielder to Jesus!" Scott says.

The Newine got its name from Acts 2:13 ("These men are full of new wine," mockers said of the apostles who were full of the Holy Spirit). "Headquarters is Love Inn, a simple barn at Freeville, New York, near Ithaca. A couple of years ago it attracted only horses, cows, and chickens. Scott Ross, with the aid of friends, turned it into a Christian coffee house that has attracted people from many states. Hitchhikers and others — the long-haired and short-haired, hippies and straights — come with sleeping bags, and some with no sleeping gear, to sleep on the floor of a crowded house adjacent to the barn, or on the barn floor itself. They are drawn, asserts Scott, by the same Spirit, and the lost become found!

"A young girl who heard the Love Inn Company [now Newine] in Maryland left home and hitchhiked five hundred miles, alone, for more of this life in Christ that until then had been no more than a dream," Scott recalls. "She was returned to her parents but not until the seed of a new Life was planted within her in the person of Jesus Christ."

But Scott Ross' big outreach is once again through radio — this time for his Lord who transformed his

Disc Jockey on a New Trip • 57

life. It began with a meeting in early 1970 with Pat Robertson, president of The Christian Broadcasting Network, and Larry Black, producer and salesman with CBN. They prayed about the unreached millions who are unaware of Jesus Christ, and talked about the drug problem. Out of it came the syndicated "Scott Ross Show." Beamed exclusively to rock lovers, it is definitely atypical of evangelical musical programs. It is heading for top rock stations not only in the U.S. but in other lands as well. Using top rock tunes and songs with both contemporary sounds and a Biblical message, Ross keeps the ear of many youth who have either dropped out of church or have never gone. Through interviews and other talk between tunes, Ross induces listeners to consider Jesus Christ as the only source of true, lasting satisfaction and the Man who can supply the kind of love that will solve the problems the Now Generation seeks solutions to.

Because of some of Scott Ross' way-out methods, not all evangelical ministers are in sympathy with his program. But one pastor who doesn't see eye-to-eye with Scott says that, while he can't go along with his music and some of the things he says, Scott is catching the ear of young people he would have no opportunity of reaching.

Anxious to see the cause of Christ advance, Ross has criticized ministers for their lack of vision and action in getting the Gospel out of the church to those who have no inclination toward church attendance. Sometimes in his criticism of the church he hasn't been careful to distinguish between the liberal and evangelical church, an evangelical pastor commented.

58 • UNHOOKED

For these reasons and others, Scott Ross is a controversial figure. But Ross apparently isn't worried. He believes he's doing his thing the way God wants him to do it. Time will tell if he should make adjustments. One thing is sure — he is not the same deejay and emcee who once worked in and around New York City. The drug habit is behind him and he's full of the Spirit, he'll tell you, and no longer controlled by marijuana or LSD. As a result, he's on the greatest trip of his young life, a happy victim of the "new wine" of Acts 2.

6. GEORGE BALLA'S LAST GREAT TRIP

by Betty Swinford

A bottle of wine. Speed. LSD. Marijuana. It was Saturday, November 16, 1968, and George Balla, nineteen, was preparing for a trip to end all trips. Either it would be so fantastic that he could boast of it from then on, or he would never return at all. Anything could happen. He could freak out. He could blow his mind and end up in a mental institution. He could die.

George well knew the possibilities, but it didn't make any difference. It was part of his pact with the devil, you might say. Though George was raised in a Christian home and taken to church, he had rebelled during his teen years. His garb and long hair announced to the world that he had joined the well-known clan called *hippies*.

Sick of the straight life of his childhood, he had rejected Christ and everything for which He stands. Desire to see what Satan could offer became uppermost in his heart, and he was willing to go to the bottom if need be to see if the world could satisfy.

Because of its wide usage and easy availability in Phoenix, George had started with marijuana. After being high on marijuana time after time, however, he wanted to try other things, stronger things. Speed was next. Then he began to mix and experiment, adding alcohol, sometimes taking everything at once. He went higher and higher, but each time he came down there was only emptiness gnawing at his heart and the desire to go yet higher, to get more thrills, to be satisfied.

He and a buddy went into drugstores and, between buying and stealing, obtained enough pills for cheap trips. George once took twenty-one capsules of an over-the-counter medication. Twenty minutes after he washed down the capsules with Coke, terrifying sensations took hold of him, and he went out of his head. Later he came down to earth.

His appearance went steadily downhill. Unwashed and smelly, he took his friends home with him. His mother, a godly woman who was constantly praying behind the scenes, tolerated the other hippies that came, and never once did she refuse her son entrance into their home.

Under the influence of LSD, George attributed to himself all the qualities of a superman. This was life. This was real! He felt himself shaking hands with the true George Balla, and nothing mattered now except the world of drugs. Nothing else had meaning.

A leader among his own kind, George told his friends, "Grass is fine, but speed is better. And LSD is better yet. Fantastic! Better than all else put together." And he knew that in a short time he would lay all these drugs aside for the hard stuff, heroin.

His favorite psychedelic music came from the

George Balla's Last Great Trip • 61

late Jim Hendrix, a Negro singer who recently died from an overdose of drugs. To imitate his idol George grew a long moustache, which he parted in the middle and brought in downward twists.

His father all but lost hope for him. But when George would return home, no matter what the hour, a light was burning. He deeply scorned his parents' religion; yet he came home for food and sleep. Always George was aware that he was spiritually lost, that he was headed down a one-way road, that he had no hope.

On occasion the Holy Spirit spoke to him, but George closed his mind — even while his heart told him that there was nothing without Christ.

Then came that great last trip. Considering the mixture George had prepared, his great trip was most likely to end at the morgue. He had in his possession more than a half bottle of wine, a benny, marijuana, and plenty of codeine and acid. He planned to take twice as much acid and codeine as usual, though one hit of each had given him good trips before.

Since a doper rarely trips alone, George planned this trip with a friend. Their room was set up for trips and had been exciting and thrilling in times past. It had psychedelic posters on the walls with black light to show them off. Many blinking lights of different colors added to the weird beauty. When he was under the influence of drugs, the lights and pictures would further captivate his mind and even heighten the hallucinations. The two young men tripped together that night.

Early in the morning, stoned out of his mind, George started for home. He should have come

62 • UNHOOKED

down, but he hadn't. It was 6:30 on a Sunday morning. The streets of Phoenix were deserted. It was chilly. The sun had come up but there seemed to be a gray mist hanging over the world.

The more he walked, the colder he became. He was hungry. Such misery gnawed at him as he had scarcely ever known. He'd taken his mixture of drugs and wine. He'd had the lights and the hallucinations. He'd been on his great trip. But things were far from right.

George was worried. He'd dropped LSD about 7:00 o'clock the evening before, and he should be down by now. Instead, he felt very strange. He wasn't going to be like this permanently, was he?

Brain damage! Maybe he *had* flipped! Maybe he had come down and didn't even know it! His head seemed to sway three feet from side to side and it felt enormous. He wanted desperately to wad himself into a ball and die. He felt that his brain was scrambled. Sights and sounds did not go together, everything was jumbled. Fear swept over him, and he cried out from within, admitting to himself at last that he was without hope.

Just as suddenly the voice of the Holy Spirit, put aside for so long that his conscience had become numbed, began to speak again. There was an urgency about that quiet voice now. It was as though the heavens had opened, and God was extending His hand once more to George Balla, dirty, smelly, rebellious hippie. God's presence was acutely real. Now! It was now, on the streets of Phoenix. He must not delay!

George heard himself begin talking to God. "I

George Balla's Last Great Trip • 63

know I need help. I know I can't do anything by myself."

Speaking aloud, George ignored the fact that people were beginning to stir about. A couple of paperboys came along. By now George had begun to cry. "God, if You still want me, if You're still interested in me, will You please help me? W—will You please — save me?"

All the desperation of a human heart was wrapped up in that cry, and the change was immediate. "For whosoever shall call upon the name of the Lord shall be saved" (Rom. 10:13). The presence of God enveloped George utterly, hovering about him during the fifteen-minute walk home.

He had begun to improve as soon as he received Christ, and by the time he walked through the front door of his home George was almost himself.

The light had burned through the night hours and was still on, a welcome signal. He went to his room and was debating whether to bathe for church or take a nap first when his mother walked in. The pain showed in her eyes, and George began to tell her that he'd met Jesus Christ. But after the first two words he began to sob, and the two of them wept together. His father was awakened and deeply touched by the change in his son. A true prodigal had come home.

George saw himself in the bathroom mirror that morning as a smelly, filthy, unshaven bum. It was a shock to him to fully realize what he looked like.

It was necessary for George to go to church with long hair that day, but he was clean and shaved. The next day a friend came to the house and cut his hair. A symbol to George of his old life, the

64 • UNHOOKED

long hair had to go, and he didn't even want to wait until Tuesday when the barber shops would open.

His devotion to sin had led him to the very brink of self-destruction. It had broken his mother's heart and bowed his father's spirit. Only the grace of God and the love of Jesus Christ had brought him through to life instead of death.

There was no doubt about it now. By God's grace his real last great trip still lay ahead; it was going to be a lifelong walk of devotion to his Lord.

A P.S. by George Balla

It was after the original account was written by Betty Swinford that I lost the control of my mind for a while. In Phoenix at that particular time (December '68) there was quite an outbreak of Hong Kong flu. The Teen Challenge Center, where I was at the time, was hit with it also, and the side effects were rather unusual for me.

Any food that I would try to take into my system would either regurgitate or run right through it and I became dehydrated. The effects of all the different kinds of drugs I had taken began to affect my thinking and I was frequently completely "out of my head" and didn't even know who I was.

For a period of days at a time I would be lost from reality in what seemed to be a hopeless way. I was convinced in my mind (at times) that my soul had left my body, and that I was doomed to die an insane man . . . cut off from the land of the living. Doctors told my folks that a "chronic brain syndrome" was causing the trouble and that there was no cure known to medical science.

George Balla's Last Great Trip • 65

But prayer won out! Because of the faithful prayers of concerned saints, the Lord Jesus Christ once again delivered me from all my fears and delusions. Believe me, I hadn't *wanted* to "trip" again . . . it seemed for a time that the work of rebuilding that the Lord had begun had been ruined. We know that the devil desired to "sift me like wheat" but the Lord restored my faith.

In the months since then my mind has been cleared in a thorough way. Time after time the Holy Spirit has blessed my efforts to communicate Christ to others.

The first miracle was His saving my soul; the second one is His continued leading and guiding. Now I have the same battles that other Christians fight. No longer is it the urge to get "stoned" but the daily fight against the weapons that the enemy of our souls uses — such as the "world," the "flesh," and numerous other deceiving devices.

This is my witness — I have an experience in Christ that nothing can equal, not even for a little while — not since I have committed my path to the Lord!

For a year the Lord has made me feel at home in the Teen Challenge Institute of Missions in Rhinebeck, New York, where young people from all over the nation train to go into the world to spread the Gospel. It differs from other Bible schools because of the backgrounds of the folks here. But praise the Lord! We are all brothers and sisters in Christ, and our goal is to know Him better, to be able to hear His voice when He makes His will known.

7. BREAKAWAY

by Lon Gregg

as told to James R. Adair and Stanley Baldwin

I remember the first time I smoked grass. It was a deliberate, well-thought-out act. After all, I was a collegian, not some junior high kid looking for kicks. Indeed, my performance was straight enough back in junior high to earn me the office of student body president.

I did all right in high school too: president of my junior class, three years on the student council, winner of a $2,400 first year scholarship to Dartmouth.

Oh, I suppose a psychologist might trace my troubles back to those days. I was pretty much taken with a nonconformist English teacher, a cotroversial character who got in trouble with some narrow-minded people (like my folks) for using a bad word in class. Some of the books I read then, by Ayn Rand and others, helped determine the set of my sails too — away from God.

I really liked Dartmouth at first. There was an earnestness about life. My fellow students didn't seem to dillydally with their studies as high school kids do. There were many discussions among us about involvement and commitment and other idealistic concepts. I felt that my life had started over in some crucial way.

"A new start for me, Lon Gregg" — I don't know how many times I thought that's what I had, when all the time I was the same old disintegrating person.

Well, as I said, smoking grass was a deliberate choice. I'd been thinking about it for a long time. It didn't look to me as if it was going to be harmful, and guys said it expanded their minds. I figured grass could make me a better person. I can see now that maybe I was only rationalizing, but then I told myself it was good. That was at Christmastime 1967.

Marijuana is relatively mild. I thought that in some way it did open a new door to me, that something was really there. I smoked it about once a week during the next term. Then I tried mescaline, a relatively mild hallucinogenic. With that, it was a struggle to keep my composure and sense of self-control.

For some reason I became very despondent during that term of school. I mean, it got bad enough so that I thought about taking my life if things didn't improve. Finally I went to the college psychiatrist. "This is really it; from now on I'll change," I thought. Six times I went and he cheered me up. He would give me a little commonsense advice that sounded to me like a bolt out of the blue, really *truth*. Of course it was truth, but somehow with each visit it seemed less and less the adequate answer.

Then summer came and with it another "new start." I began selling dictionaries. I didn't take the job for the money but strictly for the self-improvement. The manager presented it that way, as a plan

68 • UNHOOKED

to make one a much stronger person. They had all sorts of mental self-help, positive thinking, and draw-on-the-power-within-you programs. I decided this was more promising than my psychiatric treatments. I was actually looking for salvation through selling!

Mononucleosis stepped in before I could run that thread of hope to its end. I got well in time to start school again that fall with a term in France. Hashish was very easy to buy in Paris and inexpensive. Many of my fellow students had never smoked or taken drugs, but they turned on to the hashish.

By now, it had become apparent to me that drugs could not expand the mind because a drug could not really add anything that was not already there. It might help bring out what was there, however, and in me that was inadequacy. In France, then, I wasn't really looking for mind expansion; instead the drug experience became a fraternal thing or a conspiratorial thing. We were like a Satanic fellowship. It was tied in with freaky rock music that was no longer really rock music but biological rhythm, a religious kind of thing.

The impact of this whole package was exhilarating. We seemed to have a wonderful new youth culture that was a radical and real departure from what had gone before. I remember thinking, "Wow, if this really happens, we will be the first generation in the history of mankind to really break away clean. All others have gone through the oedipal struggle only to accept at last the ways of their fathers." It was exciting to me.

Then I broke my ankle while skiing. A French girl I met consoled me. She was from a strong Roman Catholic background, but within a month her ideas changed completely, and she would visit me overnight two or three times a week.

Later the same year when I returned to Dartmouth I started using LSD. I found it much stronger than marijuana or mescaline. And it was different. Afterward I remarked that it was a religious experience. I couldn't say *how* it was religious except that I could seem to sense a basic dualism in me — right and wrong warring against each other.

I had long since discounted religion but now found my interest rekindled. I began reading about Oriental religions. I also got engrossed in a book called "Revolution for the Hell of It." It's author, Abbie Hoffman, founder of the Yippies, became my hero. I had met Hoffman when he came to Dartmouth to speak. Weird! When we were introduced, the guy just stood and stared at me for about ten seconds. I was enchanted and soon began to adopt his anarchist views. Hoffman believed there was no meaning in life except what we made ourselves in any way we could. Actually I was going off in two directions at the same time: renewing an interest in religion and yet buying the philosophy that life was meaningless. No wonder I was fragmented.

Then came my bad LSD trip, my terror, my private hell. I faced the worst thing imaginable, the vacuum in the center of my being. The whole, awful truth slammed home to me that at the very base of my existence there was nothing.

A girl was tripping with me. Her face changed back and forth before my eyes from an angelic to a devilish appearance. I tried to stop it, but failed. The floor began to smoke. I staggered out into the hall and it was tilting back and forth, and rising and falling like the deck of a ship. At the same time it was stretching and distorting as if it were made of rubber. But the worst thing of all was this total unrelatedness and emptiness I felt.

Afterward I actually prayed. I can't remember the words. Driven to this low, low estate, I had to turn to something. I had planned to drop out of school and join a hippie community, but my bad trip shook me so seriously I changed my mind.

I was still very far from knowing God. Yet after that prayer the vacuum was replaced with some irreducible something. Maybe I had experienced a birth of faith. Anyhow, I wrote myself a note, headed it "Sacred Vow" and inscribed it with, "You've got to do this: — say a prayer every night."

I knew there was no way I could relate to God. No way. But I wanted to do something, and even if it were meaningless I thought at least the experience of praying might blossom into something. So I prayed for three weeks. Night after night I prayed to the walls! But it didn't blossom into anything and there was never a glimmer of an answer. After all, how could there be when there was no God?

My prayers had accomplished nothing, but I now began to read an old twenty-cent Bible I had picked up at a book sale after my bad trip. Since summer was beginning, I also decided to try selling the dictionaries again. After all, I had not completely exhausted that thread of hope. Six weeks later, I had. I felt I was deceiving both myself and my customers by trying to be sold on the books. As this feeling grew, my sales efforts slumped. I spent my time reading the old Bible and my revolutionary materials instead of working.

Finally, I chucked the dictionaries, packed my few things in a duffle bag, and hit the road. I drifted around the country from Nebraska to Colorado to California and back to Colorado, reading the Bible more and more.

I decided to withdraw from college because I knew it was useless to continue. I traveled to Hanover, New Hampshire, to Dartmouth, made my action official, and moved into a little cabin in the woods near Hanover. I worked some to pay my debts and spent most of my free time reading the Bible.

Then, I withdrew even more. Taking only my Bible and a sleeping bag, I hiked deeper into the woods. For a week, I went without food and spent all my time reading the Bible.

For the first time I read the Gospels: Matthew, Mark, Luke, and John. A story of an encounter between Jesus and a rich young man got hold of me. "What must I do to gain the Kingdom of Heaven?" the young man asked.

Jesus said, "Repent, sell all you have, and follow Me."

I decided that was my answer too, and that I would do what Jesus told him to do. I had used drugs and lived in immorality with several girls, so I swore off both. I had already given up all my possessions. All that remained was to follow Christ; as best I knew how, I determined to do that.

Some time later I was walking the mile from town to my cabin one night when a strange thing happened. The path ahead of me seemed light somehow. Twice I actually stopped and turned on the trail to see if there was someone behind me with a light. When I reached the top of the hill, the wind was blowing like crazy in the leaves up there. Maybe the wind was blowing everywhere, and I suppose it was. But there had been no wind blowing while I walked up, and I had never seen it blow on this hilltop before. Anyway, by now I was trembling, sure that God was there. I fell to my knees and reaffirmed my determination to follow Him.

I was still far from understanding how the things I read in the Bible all fit together, but I struck out on faith for the moratorium scheduled in Washington, D.C. I don't know exactly why I went; I was still searching.

With only my Bible, a sleeping bag, and three dollars, I headed south. People who picked me up on the road gave me lodging a couple of nights. I told them all I could about religion. "That's where the answer is," I declared. I even told one family that I thought I was a prophet of some kind. "Don't you think the message of Jesus is for everyone?" I asked.

They turned out to be Jewish. "Who are you to come into our house and tell us such things?" they asked angrily.

On November 14, 1969, the day before the moratorium, I reached Washington. There were workshops and group gatherings all over the place, and I wandered from one to another. At the Radical Religious Action workshop, where some were vowing to fall on the soldiers' bayonets if it came to that, I again committed myself to follow the will of God.

Then I found some Yippies and ran through the streets with them for a while. Many of them were on drugs and shouting obscenities, and I knew that was wrong so I dropped out.

Next I got into a group called The International Society for Krishna Consciousness. These yellow and orange robed people who had shaved their heads danced to the beat of drums and chanted:

> "Hare Krishna Hare Krishna
> Krishna Krishna Hare Hare
> Hare Rama Hare Rama
> Rama Rama Hare Hare!"

(This movement began in 1966 in New York City. Its founder is Indian religious leader Prabhupada A. C. Bhaktivedanta Swami. The Krishna followers believe their Hare Krishna chant reawakens the link between God and man that is dormant in everyone.)

I soon moved on, unmoved by the chanters. Some college kids were handing out a booklet called "The Four Spiritual Laws." "They are getting close," I thought, "but I had the *real* experience out in the woods."

Another fellow was handing out pictures of Christ, and underneath was printed, "A wanted Christ — Revolutionary." Below that was a lot of anarchistic, radical, revolution propaganda. It was signed at the bottom: Committee for Absolute Revolution. I thought it was great.

There were many more groups. There were Veterans for Peace, Socialists for Peace, Communists for Peace, and Homosexuals for Peace. Groups as opposite as Black Panthers and White Supremacists marched for peace. Somewhere along the line I realized something. Get four hundred thousand people together marching for peace, and all individual identity is lost. Let them go back home, however, and they are the same bitter, unhappy, prejudiced people as always. They are at war within and with one another. What is this peace for which they march?

But I didn't see it then. I thought I was doing the will of God in promoting revolution.

After the moratorium, I drifted down to Leesburg, Virginia. A friendly fellow picked me up and took me to his home. When he found out I was a radical and religious, he became unfriendly on both accounts. He was a good, straight, all-American drunk. He got so plastered that he even struck his wife and threatened to kill the children and have me arrested. Meanwhile, the drunk's family turned out to be "extremely religious" as some would say. Actually they were earnest, biblical Christians.

We talked for hours about the Bible. Things were opening up for me so that I understood parts I never really saw before. Still, I was not satisfied to stay in Leesburg. I hopped a truck, headed west, and arrived in Chicago on November 20.

I went first to a place that had "Christian" in its title. I didn't know anything about the organization, but I wanted to talk with someone about Christ and this was a "Christian" group. Well, they didn't want to take in a penniless hippie, and they didn't talk about Christ either, so I moved on.

Then, I tried the Pacific Garden Mission, on South State, just south of the main business area.

As soon as I came in the door I was asked, "Do you know Christ as your personal Saviour?"

"Well, yes," I replied hesitantly.

That didn't satisfy him, and he asked me the same thing again.

Now, there was no way I could honestly answer Yes to that question because, though I was all wrapped up in my religious searchings, I didn't really know what his question meant. So, this time I said No.

They took me to the Servicemen's Center canteen, and while I ate, one of the fellows tried to explain it all to me. He said I needed to receive Christ into my heart, but I didn't understand that. Finally I knelt with him and prayed, "Christ, will You come into my heart?" But I was so mixed up, so terribly lost, that I didn't know what the words meant.

Mission leaders invited me to stay there. The next morning I was just sitting there reading my Bible when Ray Wilson came over and said, "Lon, do you think reading the Bible will bring you salvation?"

That did it. "I don't know! I don't *know!*" I cried in desperation. "What else is there? Is there still something more required — after all I've done?"

Well, Ray talked with me for maybe five minutes. It wasn't anything I had done or could do to earn my salvation, he said. It was Christ alone. I had to realize it wasn't my repentance or my "faith" or my trying to do the will of God, or anything else of myself. The Bible said the *gift* of God was eternal life through Jesus Christ the Lord.

Then it dawned on me. I had been *trying* for months, but I hadn't just trusted wholly in Jesus

76 • UNHOOKED

Christ. It was a tearful experience when I realized the truth and inwardly turned away from myself to Christ.

Ray said, "Now, Lon, according to the Bible, what gift has just been given to you?"

I said, "Eternal life," and it dawned on me that it was true! Suddenly I had peace.

Ray took me to Ruby, the lady at the reception desk and I told her, "I've just become a Christian." Again there came this wonderful, wonderful feeling of having come into a family, of having come home, of having found what I had looked for so long.

I had made a great breakaway from drugs and my old kind of life, a new start that was really new, and at last I was truly free.

The Bible describes my experience perfectly: "Therefore if any man be in Christ, he is a new creature: old things are passed away; behold, all things are become new" (II Cor. 5:17).

* * *

Lon Gregg has remained at Pacific Garden Mission, studying the Bible and relating it to himself — and witnessing to servicemen who come to the Mission's Servicemen's Center. He currently is assistant director of the Center. Recently he married Miss Janet Ziegler, the daughter of a Mission employee. Lon has been called on many times to go out to churches and other places to tell of his transforming experience.

8. QUEST FOR LOVE

by Vicky Riccardella

as told to James R. Adair and Charlene Blanchard

It was almost 3 A.M. in New York City. Reluctantly I said good-night to my boyfriend, Tasos, and hurried up the steps to my family's house. At the door I hesitated, dreading to face Mother the next day.

"Vicky," Mother would complain, "you know your father and I don't want you coming in so late. Why do you insist on disobeying? And why do you run around with those long-haired hippies? If you continue to stay with them you'll pick up their philosophy of free love. Why, already your style of clothing is far from modest!"

What does she know about love? I thought bitterly, tiptoeing to my room. *They don't really care about me. All they care about is what the neighbors will say.*

What did it matter if I stayed out late, anyway? I had plenty of free time. I was in the spring semester of my senior year at William Cullen Bryant High School. Since I had already met most of the graduation requirements, I only had to go to school four hours a day.

78 • UNHOOKED

During my free time I had met Tasos Mahairas, an eighteen-year-old Greek hippie. He became a dropout after being suspended from school because of his long hair and radical ideas. We hit it off and enjoyed smoking pot together.

I had been smoking marijuana before I met Tasos. I saw how it caused people to laugh a lot and seemingly have a good time. But I didn't want marijuana for the kick; I wanted it because I was told it would help me delve more deeply within myself. I wanted it so I could live in a more intellectual and perceptive realm. (All of this, I learned later, is just so much false propaganda.)

I had begun smoking marijuana just about every morning. I felt it made me very sensitive to other people and to their emotions. It also seemed to let me detect if someone were a hypocrite. It sort of made me listen more in school, too, but with a superior attitude.

Luckily, my parents didn't know that I was on pot. I sighed and climbed into bed. They wouldn't understand that it was helping me find myself, I told myself.

The next morning went as I had predicted. But in spite of my mother's demands, I continued seeing Tasos and often stayed out late. Finally, one day my mother blew up.

"I'm sick of your attitude!" she shouted. "I can't take it anymore. You and your attitudes and your friends are ruining Danielle [my kid sister was ten]. If you want to leave this house, you just go right ahead!"

Hoping to find love and real meaning in life, I went to live with people who appreciated my way of life. I shared a four-room apartment with Tasos, Kurt, and Tanya. We slept on mattresses on the floor and ate with chopsticks. But we didn't care; we didn't want a lot of possessions or money. All we wanted was to be ourselves, to be natural and carefree. We just wanted to groove with other people — to get together and share life.

To me, living with Tasos wasn't wrong; it was the accepted thing to do. I just couldn't see marriage. It was so phony — all the breakups and the lack of communication. . . . A marriage license seemed to be just a piece of paper to justify two people living together. If I really loved Tasos, I felt, then it didn't matter whether or not we had that piece of paper.

I hadn't been away from home very long before my parents became concerned about my living situation. Again and again they pleaded with me to come home, but again and again I refused. I wasn't going back to all those arguments. Here in my new living situation we stuck together and showed deep concern for one another. There was no generation gap.

One day Tasos and I had what we considered a significant "spiritual" experience on an LSD trip. We came off the trip and, in our confused way, began seeking a Supreme Being.

(Here I must state that LSD experiences are in no sense true spiritual experiences, the kind that puts one in touch with God. LSD cannot be considered a way to God or even a steppingstone to God — no more so than a hideous sin that causes one deep guilt and eventually a reaching out for God. LSD "spiritual" experiences are completely counterfeit, of Satan as far as I am concerned. The fact that Tasos and I eventually found God at all is wholly because He sought us and found us and brought us to Himself. That is why I share this story — to show how He rescued us from our sin and from the drug culture.)

Taking long walks in Central Park with Kurt, Tanya, and Tasos, I began to sense God in nature. I knew about God, having been raised in the Roman Catholic Church, but I had rejected the Church when I was seventeen. I concluded now, through nature, that there had to be a God. I began to feel that God must have made everything. I rationalized, therefore, that everything must be good, even the drugs I took. (Granted, certain drugs can be considered "good" in the sense that they benefit mankind when used or prescribed by trained medical men. But Tasos and I were misusing God's created resources. Our use of hallucinatory drugs, I now know, was purely self-indulgent and in the long run physically harmful — far from being of God!)

But I became worried and confused, because slowly Tasos was beginning to change. Were drugs getting to his mind?

He had read in N. Kazantzakis' *The Last Temptation of Christ* that Christ was only an ordinary man. Now Tasos was having strange dreams. When he woke up he'd believe that he was Jesus Christ. He never came out and told me that he thought he was Jesus Christ, but I knew that he started to believe it.

I knew Tasos wanted to be Christ so he could help other people. Everyone trusted him, and he really wanted to help them, but he just didn't know how. Finally, he decided that he should go to Europe and tell everybody there that there was a God who loved them. Yet he personally didn't know Him.

But Tasos never got to Europe. When his parents found out that he thought he was Jesus Christ, they committed him to a mental institution. What would happen to him? Tasos wasn't insane, just confused. "God," I prayed desperately, "I don't know who I'm praying to, but I believe You exist. Please, please keep Tasos safe from the effects of the shock treatments."

Within a few weeks Tasos was released from the mental hospital. Then he, Kurt, Tanya, and I decided to go to California. We would hitchhike, taking only what we could carry in a knapsack.

The night before we were to leave, Tanya blew her mind. She, Kurt, and Tasos had taken LSD. They had enough for me, too, but for some reason I just didn't feel secure in taking it. I knew that LSD was powerful and that one could never be sure what was to take place. I would be under LSD's influence for about ten hours and I didn't feel that I should take it that night. So I didn't.

Tanya had a bad trip. She kept saying over and over, "It's all a game; it's all a game." Then she began to think she was an atom. When Tanya came close to us we tried to tell her we loved her, but she attempted to tear out our eyes. That night she went completely insane. It didn't seem real; Tanya had taken LSD many times before and nothing like this had ever happened.

The next day, about a month before the end of school, I went back to live with my parents. I realized that I had been running from reality instead of getting closer to it.

82 • UNHOOKED

Tasos and I didn't break up right away; we continued seeing each other and had another LSD trip. This trip, however, seemed to mark the beginning of the end for our relationship. On that trip Tasos saw me as Satan; he thought that I was the devil trying to trick him. After that trip we each believed that the other was trying to be better than the other. We argued much and became increasingly cynical of one another.

Finally one day in July 1968 Tasos left me. He said he was leaving New York City to find God. He said that God would speak to him if he got away from society and went north into the woods. There God was going to tell him what he had to do here on earth.

After leaving New York City Tasos hitchhiked to Lake George, a town some two hundred miles north on a lake by the same name. Immediately he hunted out a camp nearby where he had spent the previous summer. Here he hoped to find God. However, because of his appearance, he was not allowed to stay.

Shaken in his hope of finding God, Tasos headed for the beach. Here he lived for several days with other hippies.

The day he decided to return to New York City he spent the morning softly strumming his guitar. As he played, a young man introduced himself as Bruce Wagner. He was a student at Penn State University, who also had an active interest in guitar.

As they talked, Tasos found that Bruce was also interested in spiritual experiences. But Bruce's experiences, unlike Tasos', didn't depend upon LSD or imagination. His spiritual life was centered in Jesus

Quest for Love • 83

Christ, God's Son. He said it was Christ who gave him a life full of love for God and for other people. Then he showed Tasos what God said about Him in the Bible.

At first Tasos didn't know what to make of Bruce. Because Bruce said he had the Prince of Peace in his heart, Tasos thought Bruce was the devil trying to trick him into something. His mind whirled because he had thought of himself as Christ. But the more Bruce spoke, the more Tasos began to feel he saw the truth of God in him because Jesus Christ was in him. Tasos began to realize that he himself was a phony according to God's Word.

For almost three hours Tasos and Bruce talked and took turns playing the guitar. Bruce invited Tasos to return with him to Word of Life Island about forty miles north at Schroon Lake, New York, where Bruce was a counselor. Having nowhere else to go and no ride to New York, Tasos agreed.

The speedboat ride across Schroon Lake to the island was silent except for the motor's roar and sound of splashing water. As the lights of the town of Schroon Lake faded in the distance on the mile ride to the island, Tasos remembered a dream he had had as a child. It involved an island where he would meet people who loved one another. Could this be that island?

Tasos arrived on the island with no money and no clothing other than what he wore. But in the next days the campers — high schoolers and collegians — took care of him. They fed him and shared clothing with him.

Tasos spent a week listening to speakers and reading and discussing the Bible. He discovered that Jesus Christ had come to earth and lived a perfect life. Then He had died as a sacrifice for man's sin and had risen from the dead.

If he, Tasos, would admit to God his sin and helplessness to do good, and would accept Jesus' death as making him right in God's sight, then he would have eternal life and Christ would make him into a new person. At the end of that week, Tasos did trust Christ as his Saviour, and became a transformed person.

About two weeks later, he called me in New York. I was so mad at him for not calling sooner that I began scolding him. When I cooled off, he broke the news. "I have found what I have been looking for. Please, Vicky, come up here to Schroon Lake and find what I have found. Everybody is praying for you."

I arrived at Schroon Lake about midnight that Friday. Nervously, I walked into the bus station — sort of a pizza place — to phone Word of Life Island. Just as I hung up I heard someone call my name. Quickly I spun around. There, standing in the doorway holding my suitcases, was Tasos. I didn't recognize him at first; he had shortened his once shoulder-length hair and he radiated a new personality.

As I followed Tasos and the counselor with him down to the speedboat, Tasos tried to explain to me what had happened to him. He was so nervous and excited, though, that he didn't quite know how to go about it. He kept telling me he was going to give me a Bible — and the counselor kept telling him to take it easy, because I didn't understand what he was trying to say.

Quest for Love ● 85

I loved that island from the very beginning. Never had the stars seemed so brilliant as they did there that night. The people, too, were simply tremendous. The boys were real gentlemen! And the girls took care of me and even gave me some of their clothes.

That night before I went to bed, Tasos told me, "Vicky, just open your eyes, your ears, and your heart to everything here. You will find the truth."

The next morning after breakfast, Tasos and I went down to the dock to talk. Here he took out his Bible and began to show me from it that I was a sinful person, and that I needed to be saved.

But I didn't understand. "What does 'saved' mean?" I asked him. "What does it mean to be saved? What do I have to be saved from?" Then he explained to me the Four Spiritual Laws.

Suddenly it hit me hard: God had loved me all this time! He had a purpose for my life, but I had been out of touch with Him because of my sin, and so I couldn't really know Him.

When I realized how wretched I must be in God's sight, I cried for the longest time.

Tasos explained further why God had sent Christ to earth, and I accepted the fact that Christ had paid the penalty for my sin. Then I prayed and asked Christ to please rule my life from then on.

Tasos and I spent the rest of the summer working in the dining hall on the island. Two weeks before we were to leave, Jack Wyrtzen (Word of Life director) asked me what I was going to do in September. "I don't know," I told him. "I've been praying all summer that God would show me what

86 • UNHOOKED

He wants." Jack suggested that Tasos and I talk to Dr. Bob Jones, Jr., who was then on the island.

Dr. Jones accepted both Tasos and me to enter Bob Jones University in Greenville, South Carolina, that September. We are now in our junior year there.

Right now Tasos and I really aren't sure what God wants us to do with our lives. After we gave our lives to God, He changed our whole way of thinking. Now, whatever we do, we just want to work for Him.

* * *

Since this story was written, God has continued to work in the lives of Vicky and Tasos. They have discovered the wonder of romance without drugs and, as this book is about to be published, they plan to be married in June 1971. "We want to spend our summer working as missionaries in New York City," reports Vicky.

9. MONKEY OFF MY BACK

by Herb Green

I began smoking marijuana and taking pills as a teen-ager in high school in East Orange, New Jersey, during 1945. I was a troublemaker in school, and eventually dropped out to join the Marine Corps in 1946. I came home in 1948 to find most of my friends using heroin. I first began by sniffing and then I graduated to the hypodermic needle. I didn't realize that this was the beginning of ten years of hell on earth.

Stealing and conning people was the order of the day. Sometimes I found myself shooting up to fifty dollars a day. I had a girl friend who was also a drug addict and a prostitute, and through her prostitution and my selling drugs we managed to support our habit, which was beginning to eat away at my life. I soon lost about fifty pounds, becoming nothing but skin and bones. During these horrible ten years I was in and out of jails and prisons. Many of my personal friends died from overdoses of narcotics, and I had many close calls myself.

In spite of all this I continued to use drugs, for there seemed to be no other life for me. I talked to doctors and psychiatrists in a vain and futile effort to free myself from the hell and punishment

88 • UNHOOKED

which was taking its toll on my life. I joined Narcotics Anonymous and other rehabilitation programs, but to no avail.

After serving two years in a federal prison for selling drugs, I gave up all hope concerning rehabilitation. In prison I learned the confidence game and many other schemes to get money, and so I became a hardened criminal besides being a junkie. I began believing that the only way for me to rid myself of the drug habit was to accidentally take an overdose! Believing these lies kept me chained to my fears and doubts. I believed that the only way to enjoy myself was to destroy myself. I believed once a drug addict always a drug addict. I believed that because I was a black man I couldn't make it in this society. Worst of all, I believed that God had made me to be what I was, a failure.

There is an expression — "the monkey on your back" or "the vulture on your veins." This became a startling reality to me. Sometimes I awoke in the middle of the night and felt the spirit of a monkey clinging to my shoulders with its legs while choking me with its hands. I would struggle trying to breathe until this thing would release me. I didn't dare tell anyone about this, not even my junkie friends, afraid I would be put into a mental institution.

When I got strung out on drugs and couldn't get a fix I would be in a tormented state, physically and mentally. The human body by nature releases a fluid which lubricates the joints, but when the addict is really hooked the heroin replaces this fluid, and the fluid ceases to function properly. Therefore the withdrawing addict gets an awful ache in

Monkey Off My Back • 89

his back and other parts of the body. Usually after three or four days of cold turkey this fluid returns to its normal function. This is what we call "paying the dues." Besides my numerous aches and pains, I was nervous and fidgety and experienced an awful itching in the pit of my stomach. I broke out in cold sweats and experienced countless sleepless nights.

Sometimes I tried to pray, but it seemed as if the heavens were made of brass. But thanks to God, my Christian mother often knelt at the foot of my bed and prayed until tears streamed down her face, pleading for God to have mercy on me. However, I was stubborn and rebellious, and I couldn't stand for my mother to pray. "Leave me alone!" I would scream hysterically. "Get out of my room!"

I had all kinds of preconceived ideas about the church and many false concepts about God, because I had seen so much hypocrisy among so-called Christians. Therefore I was leery when God or church was suggested as the answer to my problems.

Over a period of ten years my mother spent nearly $2,000 on lawyers, bondsmen, and hospital fees, trying to assist me in whatever way she could. She kept telling me that Christ was my only hope, but I just couldn't seem to accept this. In her all-out effort to see me free from drugs, my mother solicited prayer for my condition, from every Christian she came in contact with.

One evening in March 1958 one of her friends called me on the telephone, and began to tell me how much God loved me and cared for me. I concluded this woman was some kind of religious fanatic, because as far as I was concerned God hated me because I was a drug addict. But this woman's voice was soft and kind, and she was not condemning me. Instead she was showing me love and compassion, and this was what I desperately needed. She invited me to her home for prayer. Ordinarily I would have immediately rejected her invitation, but because of the love of God I sensed in this woman's voice I agreed to come.

That Monday night at her home I found Christians that were more concerned about my life and destiny than I was myself, and this impressed me deeply. They opened the Bible and convinced me that Jesus Christ could give me a positive cure. They asked me to get on my knees and pray, but I didn't know how to pray. So I mumbled a few words. Nothing happened. But I knew these people had something I wanted because I felt better by just being in their presence. They invited me back again the following Monday night. I learned later that they fasted several days for my recovery.

That next Monday night found me sick and in desperate need of a fix, and I was reluctant to go to the meeting, for I didn't want these nice people to see me sweating and vomiting. But I had promised them, and something was pushing me to go just as I was, sickness and all. I had no idea of the dramatic change that was to take place.

Once again the Christian group asked me to get on my knees and pray. Still I did not know how to pray, so I just called on the Lord and asked Him simply to save me from destroying myself and give me a new life. I was desperate and it seemed that if He didn't save me right then I would die there on my knees. I never dreamed God could answer prayer so quickly. Immediately I began to feel a burning and soothing sensation penetrate my entire being. Instantly the pain and ill feelings of withdrawal left me. It was a miracle! I leaped to my feet and began thanking God out loud, while the Christians were still on their knees praying, unaware that God had answered their prayer so quickly. A tremendous love and compassion for every human being flooded my soul, and I knew without a doubt that God had visited me.

As I walked home with my mother I noticed that the trees and the streets looked brand new to me — everything seemed to take on a new look. Later I discovered II Corinthians 5:17 and I knew why: "If any man be in Christ, he is a new creature: old things are passed away; behold all things are become new." That night I had the best night's sleep I had ever had.

But Satan wasn't giving up on me. The next day the tempter came to me and said, "Your experience last night was just a religious phenomena. You've got to get some drugs." The words were not audible, but I got the message clearly. And though I felt no need for drugs, I set out to obey. I went to a friend in East Orange who was a dealer. He was bagging up heroin at the time. I bought a five dollar bag and dumped the whole thing in the cooker and then hit myself in the left arm. A strange thing happened; I couldn't even get a buzz or a tingle. I felt absolutely nothing. I got discouraged, so I bought another bag and this time put the whole bag in my right arm. The same thing happened; I got nothing! He was sitting there nodding, not knowing what was happening to me. After kicking it back several times, I took the needle out and laid it on the table and just sat there bewildered. As I sat there, I heard a still small voice inside of me and it was God! That voice said to me, "Son, I have set you free from the narcotics habit."

Right then an awful feeling of condemnation came over me as I realized I had allowed myself to be deceived again by the forces of evil. I left that house quickly and went home. I fell on my knees and asked God to forgive me. As I wept and prayed, I felt an assurance that has never left me nor forsaken me.

This happened over thirteen years ago, and since that time I have had no reoccurrences or relapses, because Jesus Christ said, "If the Son therefore shall make you free, ye shall be free indeed" (John 8:36). Thank God I don't have to stand on street corners and meet in alleys anymore trying to make connections, for I made one connection with the Holy Spirit which is sufficient to last me for eternity. Whether you are on drugs or not, without Christ you are empty inside and you will continually turn to substitutes and imitations in an effort to satisfy the vacuum which exists in every human heart. The fulness of life is not found in religions and churches, for Christ declared, "I am come that they might have life, and that they might have it more abundantly" (John 10:10).

* * *

Since his conversion to Christ and release from narcotics, Herb Green has been ordained and preaches as the director of Ambassadors for Christ (27 N. 17th Street, East Orange, N.J. 07017). The ministry is "designed to reach all nations with a positive message

Monkey Off My Back • 93

of deliverance for body, soul, and mind through faith in the Gospel of Jesus Christ," according to Mr. Green. The group is presently engaged in a prison ministry to both men and women in the Essex County Penitentiary in Caldwell, New Jersey, a ministry to teenagers and drug addicts, a ministry of personal evangelism through street meetings and literature, and a ministry of foreign missions in Kenya, East Africa.

10. FOR BETTER—FOR SURE

by Esther Indelicato

". . . What God hath joined together let not man put asunder." With these words Joe and I were married on August 24, 1968.

It was nothing short of a miracle for both of us. In time past both of us had ridiculed marriage. "Marriage is a crutch for the neurotic," Joe scoffed. I spat words just as harshly: "I don't want to be tied down to some creep and be slave to a gang of kids."

Even before Joe and I knew each other, evil forces worked against the possibility of our divinely appointed marriage coming to pass. We were our own worst enemies, and it's a wonder one or both of us didn't die before God brought us together in marriage. Why? Primarily because Joe and I were drug addicts! While God was tenderly calling us to Himself and to each other, we were fighting Him each step of the way, heading for an empty, meaningless, self-destroying existence.

As a child I set my heart on a theatrical career. My youthful experiences revolved around glamorous toy dolls, movie magazines, and other forms of self-glorification. I wanted to have my way and do my "thing" no matter what. The so-called glamor of the stage and the bright lights were my goal. My parents catered to my dreams, giving consent to my visions of being a star.

After a series of off-Broadway shows and bit parts, I found myself teamed in 1958 with a handsome, egotistical dancing partner. We received professional acclaim and bookings. Yet I began to have moments of doubt about the value and permanence of my career. I became overanxious to secure this life for myself and insure our career and keep our partnership from coming apart. I embarked on a determined course which would end, I hoped, in marriage to my dancing partner. Subconsciously I feared losing what we had together. Humanly I fell in love with my stage partner. My spirit was aglow with all the excitement and surety of our career.

Then the curtain of my life's drama came down rudely. My dancing partner, I learned through a bitter experience, was a philanderer and had no intention of ever getting tied down with me. In an outburst of rage and unmanliness, he bruised me in spirit, mind, and body, and walked out of my life.

Like many glamor seekers who reach moments of crisis, I reacted by trying to take my own life. In an almost hypnotic trance, I reached out for a bottle of sleeping pills and took an overdose. Now I would show the whole world! Now I would bare my burdened soul in the "highest" form of self-glorification, *suicide!* Instead of waking to an Alice-in-Wonderland existence or a never-ending theaterland for broken hearts, I was once more rudely brought back into conscious reality. I proceeded in ensuing weeks to become hooked on drugs and live a life given over to Satan.

96 ● UNHOOKED

This darkness in my life culminated on February 14, 1964, at the Supreme Court in Queens County, New York, where I was arraigned on a 37-count indictment. Again overwhelmed by the burden of my setbacks, I attempted to take my life. This time in front of the judge I collapsed into unconsciousness brought on by an overdose of drugs. Later as the light of day seeped into my being and I opened my eyes, there was something different. There seemed to be a glowing warmth about me I had never known before. As I forced open my eyes, I saw blurry outlines of two figures. Two women were passing my hospital bed. Though they seemed far away, I noticed one of the women carrying a book which, unlike the blurry forms, was clearly discernible. It was a Bible. I feebly formed my lips, trying to speak. As though someone was helping me, I asked the woman, "Pray for me." Then I slipped into contented unconsciousness.

After a miraculous recovery and a series of God-directed circumstances, I was guided to David Wilkerson's Teen Challenge Center in New York City. At the Center on March 24, 1964, I saw myself as God saw me — a wretched sinner. I realized the foolishness of my ways. I sought forgiveness of God, whom I had so offended. I made my commitment and confession to Christ, my Saviour, and He became real in my life. I experienced the quickening of the Holy Spirit and the indwelling of the living God.

Some say opposites attract. In certain ways Joe and I are opposites. But without Jesus Christ we were alike. Without Him we were both hopeless and helpless.

For Better — For Sure • 97

Joe also was scarred by the indelible experiences of his youth. At fourteen in his Jamaica, Long Island, tenement-type environment, he was most concerned about being accepted by the crowd. He didn't want to be a "chicken," so he became a mainliner right away. In his eight years as an addict and a pusher, he spent almost six years in penal institutions. In prison Joe experienced the drawing of the Lord. Most of his life he had been attracted to the religious. Once, despite his strong need for the approval of other inmates, he protected a seventeen-year-old inmate from others because this young inmate was once a Roman Catholic altar boy. Joe and he would talk about religious experiences of the past.

When Joe was out of jail he committed one robbery after another to buy "stuff" for himself and his friends. Joe was a friendly guy by nature. He would do anything for his friends. His friends would do anything for him — at least he imagined it that way.

The extent of these friendships was revealed when Joe was twenty. He and the boys had a little "shooting gallery" and were all getting high. Joe was trying hard to get their approval. He overtried. He succumbed to an overdose. His buddies tried to revive him but became scared for themselves. Picking him up, they carried him to a car and drove around, still arguing about what they should do with him. Should they dump him in the river? Take him to the woods and leave him? Finally on that winter night his buddies and friends, in the middle of a snowstorm, dumped Joe in the small yard in the front of his house. After a while Joe's father came

98 ● UNHOOKED

out to find his first-born son crumpled in a heap and stoned with an overdose and looking very much dead.

Even this experience didn't thwart the urge in Joe for drugs. One night in February 1965, while riding on the Long Island Railroad train, returning home from the big city with a half-load of heroin and high as a kite, Joe was approached by a former drug addict, then a staff member of Teen Challenge. Spotting Joe's condition and led of the Holy Spirit, he challenged Joe with the reality of Jesus Christ and his need to be born again and quickened by the Spirit of God. Convicted, Joe saw the hopelessness of his condition and the depravity of his existence. He received Jesus as his Saviour and the power to become a son of God. He knew he was born of the living Spirit of God.

It was at a minister's home that Joe and I met. We were drawn together as we began to share our faith with others. In 1968 we were married. Just as God had changed our lives and made us new creatures in Christ, so God also joined us in matrimony and gave us the new life of marital union. Old things are passed away and all things are become new! Jesus, Lord and Master, is now Lord and Master of our lives, marriage and home.

Together we presently have a ministry among drug addicts. The Lord has opened doors for us to minister in prisons and houses of detention through Ambassadors for Christ. At rallies and meetings Joe and I give testimony to the power of God in our lives. We harmonize musically as well and sing praises to the Lord and to the love of God in Christ Jesus. We rejoice in the fact that God loved us so that He gave us Jesus, that His Spirit is at work daily in our lives. This is the satisfaction we both sought but didn't find in drugs.

11. HOOKED ON MY OWN MEDICINE

by Howard Thomas, M.D.

Nine years of drug abuse had nearly ruined my personal and professional life. My family had left me, my medical practice was nearly bankrupt, and I had narrowly escaped death in several auto accidents. The most shattering experience of all was the spring morning in 1965 when two deputy sheriffs entered my clinic, put handcuffs on me, and carted me off to the neuropsychiatric hospital in Murfreesboro, Tennessee. Outraged, I demanded an explanation.

"I'm sorry, Doctor," one deputy said, "but your parents have had you committed to the hospital."

As the car sped toward the hospital, my shoulders ached from the pull of the handcuffs locked behind my back. (My shoulder muscles had drawn up and hardened from repeated drug injections.) There was also the mental torture of reliving the pattern of life that had brought me to this agonizing moment.

My experience with alcohol and drugs, like that of most people, began innocently enough. My wife Ann and I began to drink socially while I was taking premedical training at Memphis State University in the early '50s. During my internship at an Atlanta hospital, I often worked until midnight and then

Hooked on My Own Medicine • 101

drove to west Tennessee to see my father who was ill. I began taking amphetamines to stay awake on these trips. I was taking them regularly by the time I finished my internship in 1955.

I began to experiment heavily with drugs shortly after beginning my practice of medicine in a small west Tennessee town in early 1956. I remembered with delight the euphoria or "lift" amphetamines (or pep pills) had given me in previous months as I took them to stay awake. So as tiredness overtook me in my work I resorted to pills. The effect was so exhilarating that soon I found myself taking several a day. Then I found that as tolerance developed it took many tablets a day to supply my need.

My desire for this drug soon found its fulfillment by injection or "skin popping," as drug users say. This way the drug had a more profound effect. Soon I found that the amphetamines in large doses gave a frightening high, coupled with nervous shaking, so I turned to the hard drugs — Demerol, morphine, and Leritine — to produce a certain degree of rest or sedation.

Eventually I found myself hooked on Methedrine (speed) and Demerol and other narcotics.

My painful memories were interrupted as the sheriff's car pulled up at the hospital. Attendants locked me into a ward with all types of addicts and sex offenders.

Here I had plenty of time to reflect on my tragic past. When my drug problem caused my practice to fall off, I began a series of moves that in the late 1950's took me and my family to southern Arizona, where I began working as a physician for a copper mining company. This lasted only a short while, and we were on the move again.

Finally, in 1961, after hope for a medical cure of my addiction had run out, I again moved to southern Arizona, securing employment with another mining company. In my work, it really began to be a problem trying to hide the scars and needle marks on my body. In the surgical dressing room I tried either to change clothes before or after the other doctors. Then at times while assisting at surgery, I found it almost impossible to remain awake during the operation.

The chief surgeon suspected something was wrong for some months, I later learned, but it was not until an early summer day in 1962 that a real crisis came into my life that threatened my future as a practicing physician.

As had become my habit after taking drugs during the working day, I drove out of the foothills into the desert in early evening to be alone and to take more drugs to try to escape the reality of the drug addict's life as I now lived it. Surely the drug addict's life is one of the most despairing and lonely lives man knows!

This particular night I was so drugged that I drove aimlessly over the desert trails for several hours, with stops only to take more drugs. Then in the early morning hours my car sputtered to a stop and I realized I was out of gas. Here I was, hatless in the cold desert air, without food or water — and only God knew where I was. It could be days or weeks before anyone had occasion to be out in the desert wilds. So some time before sunup I began walking, taking only enough drugs to sustain my

Hooked on My Own Medicine • 103

need through the day. I had no idea which way to go but just began walking.

Later, possibly about midmorning, I noticed a low-flying small plane circling areas of the desert. Probably my car had been spotted. When the plane came my way, I hid behind the trunk of the nearest large cactus plant, not wishing to be discovered in my condition. I learned later that the chief surgeon at the hospital had called my wife when I failed to show up at work. He had sent the plane out to search for me.

I continued walking the rest of the day across the parched, arid desert. It was with great difficulty that I descended the steeply inclined wall of Rattlesnake Canyon and then scaled the opposite wall. This area, as the name implies, is heavily infested with rattlers.

It was after dark when I walked out to a blacktop road and sat down, totally exhausted. Soon a pickup truck came by, stopped, and the driver gave me a ride back into Clifton, Arizona. Sheriff's deputies welcomed me and took me to my home. Here I found all my books, pictures, and diplomas from my office in the hospital and learned from my wife that I had been fired from my job.

My parents came to Arizona and brought me back to Tennessee. My wife and children stayed in Arizona so the children could finish their school term.

I helped my father do farm work, taking only enough drugs to support my craving yet managing to keep from appearing too "dopey."

In October 1962 I began my practice in Saltillo, Tennessee, where we still live and where I have my

104 • UNHOOKED

clinic. My narcotics license had been revoked, and I was in danger of losing my license to practice medicine. A crisis was also brewing in my home life.

I desperately wanted to be a decent husband and a real father to my three growing boys but I found myself spending less and less time at home. I finally moved out of our house and began to sleep in the office. A short time later, my wife and sons went to live with Ann's mother.

In spite of all these heartaches, my addiction grew steadily worse until the day I was committed to the hospital.

Life in the hospital ward was like being in prison. Anger and shame swept over me each time I thought about the irony of my predicament: a doctor of medicine shut away in a locked hospital ward to keep him from destroying himself with drugs created to relieve man's suffering.

To get out of the locked ward for a while each Sunday, I attended a church service conducted by one of the hospital chaplains. It was in one of these services that God planted the seeds of a new life in my heart. A Negro chaplain talked about the power of Jesus Christ. He made Christ sound alive and started me thinking that maybe Jesus Christ could break the chains of my addiction.

Several weeks later, after my release, I returned to my failing practice but knew it was just a matter of time until I would reach for another injection.

At the urging of a persistent friend, I agreed to attend a Methodist layman's conference at Lake Junaluska, North Carolina. I discovered that the men who rode a chartered bus with me to the mountain retreat were different from most people I knew.

Hooked on My Own Medicine • 105

They were full of joy and they talked about Jesus. I could tell that they really knew the Lord like the chaplain at the hospital did.

After arriving at the retreat grounds, some of the men asked me to attend a prayer meeting.

I was deeply disturbed when the prayer meeting was over. I could see that these men had what I desperately needed, but I wasn't sure how to acquire it.

Walking across the conference grounds the next morning, I saw some of the men who had been at the prayer meeting. My heart was crying out for help, but I didn't say anything. A plumber, sensing my need, placed his hand on my shoulder and said gently, "Doctor, would you like to be saved?"

"More than anything else in the world," I answered.

Several of the men knelt with me under an oak tree and we prayed until Christ's peace and power flooded my soul. My chains were broken on that summer day in 1965.

I returned to Saltillo a few days later with a new joy and a new sense of mission. I was excited to start telling people how Jesus could change a human life. I was especially eager to tell my wife and children.

The day after my arrival home, I went to see my wife and sons in a nearby town. Ann was skeptical about my "change" and would not return to me.

Shocked and disappointed, I returned home and tried in the next weeks to salvage my practice.

An intense emotional craving for drugs remained for some weeks, but I began each day with the simple but earnest prayer, "Lord, help me get through this day without drugs."

As I struggled, I began to witness and began to get invitations to give my testimony in churches in the area.

I sorely missed my family and longed to give them the love and protection I had failed to give before. Just prior to one speaking occasion, I went to see my wife and asked her to go to the meeting with me. To my surprise, she consented. The Holy Spirit used my testimony that night — Ann was the first to respond when the pastor gave an invitation to those who wished to commit their lives to Christ.

This experience in a country church marked a new beginning for our home. Ann and the boys returned to Saltillo the next week to begin establishing a Christian home.

We considered leaving Saltillo because of the lingering shame, but we were convinced that God had a work for us there. Soon my practice began to grow. This opened opportunities to counsel patients who needed Christ. Ann began to witness to her neighbors. The boys trusted Christ and began to tell friends about Him.

Soon God began opening many doors for me to witness outside the clinic — preach the Gospel in churches, speak to groups in schools, colleges, PTA meetings, and club gatherings. God has sent me into many states to warn of the dangers of drug use, to attempt to lead the lost to Christ, to try to point the dejected and lonely to the joy and peace found in Jesus.

My pastor, the Rev. Ralph Duncan, and I now present a Sunday morning television program on

Channel 7, Jackson, Tennessee, titled "Christ Presented."

I teach an adult Bible class at our church and Ann plays the piano when we meet. We also have a Bible study class in our home each week.

As I look back on my many experiences, such as the desert ordeal with the exposure to the hot sun and to rattlesnakes, I thank God that His hand was even at that time extended to protect and keep. As a doctor who should have known better, my experience with drugs will, hopefully, warn and encourage young people in today's drug-crazed culture. The torment of drug addiction is no respecter of persons — and neither is Jesus Christ who set me free!

This story was adapted from an original article by Rayburn W. Ray.

12. IN FROM THE COLD

by Louis Angel Garcia

I was born in Puerto Rico and come from a poor family in the city of Mayaguez. I have five brothers and two sisters. My mother worked night and day to try to supply the needs of our family. I am also from a broken home. My mother and father are divorced, the divorce coming after my father left my mother to care for us.

Sometimes we ate only one meal a day. We slept on cots. Some mornings for breakfast we had only coffee and bread.

In 1949 my mother left Puerto Rico to start a new life in New York. She hoped to find means of support and send for us children later. My brothers and two sisters and I lived with my father and stepmother. Both were cruel to us, seemingly beating us daily. Many nights they sent us to bed without food. We had few clothes, so we had to wear the same clothing for days at a time.

I was lonely in my heart and needed someone to care for me, someone to love me, someone to help me. Many nights I would cry in bed — tears of sorrow and tears of loneliness. My only hope was that someday I would find happiness in life. I wanted to be like other children who had a family and someone to love them.

In 1950 my mother sent for us to come to New York. When we arrived at the airport it was very cold weather. An airline stewardess saw us shivering and brought us heavy blankets to keep us warm. It made me feel good to have someone help us.

I never attended school in Puerto Rico; therefore I didn't know how to read or write. (I couldn't even spell or write my own name until I was eleven years old.) When I attended school in New York it naturally was hard for me.

My mother was on relief and we got just enough money to keep us from starving. We lived in a slum area in the Bronx. I learned more from the street life than what I learned in school.

At the age of fifteen I joined a gang. I had no choice, for the only way to have protection from other boys was to join a gang. I learned many things from belonging to the gang, including how to steal a car. We used the cars we stole to transport us into the area where we were to have a gang fight. I also learned to make homemade bombs, and how to fight cruelly with guns, bats, and lead pipes. I had no love in my heart. I was full of hate and anger. I didn't care for anyone, not even for myself.

Once in a fight rival gang members attacked me with bats and pipes. I was beaten up badly. I had blood all over my face and head. I thought I was going to die, but in this condition I went back to fight with the rest of my gang. I was afraid to go to a hospital, knowing the police would find out and ask questions. One of my friends later cleaned me up and put ice on my wounds. Thank God I didn't die.

A few months after this a friend of mine offered, "Have a smoke — you need a kick!" It, of course, was not a cigarette but really a stick of marijuana. When I smoked it my whole personality, my emotions, and my thinking changed. I thought this was the answer to happiness I was searching for, but I discovered it wasn't. I would drink liquor and then take pills to see if this would help me. Again I felt the same: empty and lonely, still searching for something that I couldn't find. Then another friend told me about a drug called heroin. "Take this and you'll get so high you'll forget all your troubles. You'll get that good feeling."

Little did I know that this first shot of hard stuff more literally than figuratively, was snapping handcuffs on me and putting me in slavery. I began selling drugs to support my habit and still this wasn't enough. I had to steal and mug people. The situation grew worse and I began stealing from my own mother! I would take anything I could get my hands on to make sure I would get my next fix. I didn't care about my personal appearance; I would sleep in hallways, or any place I could find.

I went to hospitals, looking for a cure from my addiction. When I came out I returned to drugs. I was busted and had to spend many months in jail. Upon my release I again hunted up a pusher. Hooked! I couldn't escape from this thing that I had become a slave to. I tried everything that I knew of; nothing worked.

The last hospital I went to was the U.S. Public Health Service Hospital in Lexington, Kentucky. I was there for six months. Many doctors and psychiatrists tried to help me. Three days before I was released, one of the psychiatrists had a talk with me. He asked me if I believed in God. I told him, "Yes, in my own way." He then told me about Teen Challenge, the Christian center started by the Rev. David Wilkerson, and he gave me a letter of introduction to take there.

After my release from the hospital I did not go to Teen Challenge but went back to the use of drugs. Some time later I was standing on a street corner, high on drugs, when a friend of mine came up to me and began talking to me about Jesus Christ and His sacrifice on Calvary for my sins. I looked at him; he had been an addict like me, but now he looked different. He was smiling; something wonderful and good had taken place in his life. I went home that night and I thought to myself, "God, if You helped him, surely You can help me." Maybe this was the answer for my life.

The next day, a Monday in 1964, I went to Teen Challenge. I was sick and needed a shot of drugs. The Rev. Don Wilkerson (David's brother who is director of Teen Challenge) talked with me and then assigned me to a room. As I lay in bed with withdrawal pains, my thoughts were on drugs. My body was craving a fix. The Rev. John Kenzy, of Teen Challenge, brought another minister to my room. This minister who was unknown to me told me about the power of God and how Christ could heal my body and my mind and give me a new heart. I asked him to pray for me, and when he did, the power of Christ touched me and I was healed. I didn't have any more withdrawal pains.

112 • UNHOOKED

God had revealed Himself to me by healing my broken and wrecked body and my twisted mind, but I still did not have God in my life.

On the third day that I was at Teen Challenge I went to a chapel service. There I heard the Word of God being preached as I had never heard it preached before. After the sermon Don Wilkerson asked those who wanted Christ to change their lives to come forward.

I didn't go forward; being shy, I was afraid. But as I heard the fellows praying and asking God to help them, I knelt by the chair I had been sitting in. There I asked Christ to come into my heart. I asked Him to change my life and to help me. In a moment I felt a peace come into my heart. I was different; my thinking had changed. Right there I had been born again. I was a child of God, and He was my Father and I was His son! Jesus had once said, "Him that cometh to Me I will in no wise cast out" (John 6:37). I had come; He had received me. John 1:12 says, "As many as received Him to them gave He power to become the sons of God." I had received Him; I was in God's family.

After completing the Teen Challenge program in Brooklyn, I went to the Teen Challenge Training Center in Rehrersburg, Pennsylvania. There my relationship with Christ continued to grow. Here I learned to place my trust in God for everything. In the Bible classes God continued to minister to the many needs of my life. After I finished the program at the farm I came back to New York and began working at the World's Fair.

Within a short time God was going to once again change the course of my life. The Rev. Don Wilkins, one of the workers from Teen Challenge in Brooklyn, was assigned to go to San Francisco to work at the new Teen Challenge Center there. Rev. David Wilkerson had told him he could take two boys to help in the work in California. I was chosen to go and we were there for six months. I met my wife, who is a minister's daughter and who was also working at the Teen Challenge center in San Francisco. We were married in California. We left San Francisco and came back to New York and felt led of God to go to Detroit to work at the Teen Challenge center starting in that city. We worked there for one year. We again felt God's leading to come back to New York. We worked in the Brooklyn center for nine months.

I then felt God placing His call on my life to go to Bible school. Though I was afraid to go because of my educational background, God assured me that He had called me and He would help me.

I went to the Teen Challenge Institute of Missions in Rhinebeck, New York. I had had only five years of secular education — less than five really for after managing to get through fifth, sixth, seventh, and eighth grades I got thrown out of ninth grade. Like Solomon, I prayed, "God give me wisdom and understanding." God heard and opened my mind and increased my understanding. To be sure, there were many struggles, but I give God the honor and glory for helping me through school. "He makes possible what is humanly impossible."

* * *

This report was written about Louis Garcia during his Bible school training by the Rev. John Kenzy, president of Teen Challenge Institute of Missions:

114 • UNHOOKED

"When God called Louis Garcia to Bible school two and one-half years ago, Louis tearfully responded, 'But, Lord, how can I go when I can't even read or write?' He had to trust God for simple understanding like few others who have gone through T. C. I. M. With a tender love for God, Louis would lay his books open before the Lord and weep and cry until he could grasp their contents. Time was precious and he was determined to avail himself of it all.

"Louis had been a heroin addict for five years and it had taken its toll on his mind. He claimed this promise, 'If any of you lack wisdom, let him ask of God, that giveth to all men liberally . . . and it shall be given him.' Joel's prophecy came true in Louis' life: 'And I will restore to you the years the locust (drugs) hath eaten . . . and ye shall be satisfied, and praise the name of the Lord your God, that hath dealt wondrously with you: and I will pour out My spirit upon all flesh. . . .'

"Louis became a shining example of God's renewing grace by maintaining a B+ average his first four trimesters and an A- average his last two. In the midst of his travailing to know God's Word, Louis did not fail to live it — one time receiving the award for the highest Christian character on campus."

* * *

Louis continues his story:

While I was in Bible school I was a representative for the student council and also student body president.

Now I am a minister of the Gospel of Jesus Christ. God has called me to tell others who are bound by the curse of drug addiction that He can set them free and bring them from a life of bondage into a life of freedom and joy through Jesus Christ. I praise and thank God for changing and transforming my life. Once I was without hope; lost in a world of darkness. Now I can say that I have hope, joy, peace, and happiness, for God has filled the emptiness that was in my life. He has given me purpose and a new goal to live for. I found what I was searching for when I gave my life to Jesus Christ.

Once I was out in the cold, without a true friend. Now I thank God I walk in the warmth of His presence and He is to me a Friend that sticks closer than a brother. He has filled the longing in my life with His precious Holy Spirit.

And, too, I thank God for giving my wife and me a beautiful baby daughter.

I am presently working as assistant dean, counselor, and teacher at Brooklyn Teen Challenge. We have been on the staff since my graduation from Bible school in December 1968.

13. THANKS TO WENDY'S MOM

by Inmate No. M-0069,
State Correctional Institution at
Dallas, Pennsylvania

Not long ago I was addicted to morphine and other dangerous drugs. Because of my constant reckless use of these drugs and several bad LSD trips, I was slowly and painfully going insane. I had been taking drugs steadily for two years and had gotten to the point where drugs were all that meant anything. I couldn't communicate with anybody or carry on a conversation. It was as if something evil had attacked my head so that I couldn't do the things I wanted to.

My passion was for drugs, and I took any kind I could get. From using belladonna and LSD, my life and world had gone completely out of shape. Everything lost its dimensions and became flat and unreal. I was sure I was going insane. I had now become violent, and more perverse every day. My thinking was twisted. I would go into spells of deep depression. I got arrested a couple of times for using drugs but I couldn't stop or understand what was going on. God was a vague Someone I called on now and then.

Thanks to Wendy's Mom • 117

Two years ago when I first started shooting morphine, I couldn't afford to buy it. So I broke into drugstores and stole large quantities of drugs. During this time I met a girl named Wendy. She too was living out on the street and taking drugs, and we started living together. While I was going insane I never wanted Wendy around because she knew what was happening to me and tried to stop me from taking drugs. I wouldn't listen to her and when I got stoned I used to beat her and cause her a great deal of pain and suffering. But through all this she never once left me. She knew I was sick. I had overdosed four times and was so close to death once my heart stopped and I turned blue. But each time I came to she'd be right there to comfort me. I used to cry and ask her, "Why, Wendy, why!?"

It's like a miracle the way we met and the fact that she never once left me, or let me down, though she was sick a lot herself. Finally I got so bad I couldn't care for her anymore, or take living on the street, and I took her home. Her mom is a Christian and I'll never forget the night I brought Wendy home. Her mom just took us both in her arms and held us and cried, and gave thanks to the Lord. Her prayers had been answered.

With real love and concern, she showed me promises from the Bible. She read John 3:16, "For God so loved the world, that He gave His only begotten Son, that whosoever believeth in Him should not perish, but have everlasting life." She made it real personal. This was for *me*. She told me how Jesus in a person's life makes all the difference in the world. She showed me II Corinthians 5:17 telling how a person becomes all new and old things pass away when he has Christ inside. And Wendy's mother shared with me such promises for the Christian as I Corinthians 10:13: "There hath no temptation taken you but such as is common to man: but God is faithful, who will not suffer you to be tempted above that ye are able; but will with the temptation also make a way to escape, that ye may be able to bear it."

I hated my old ways; this new kind of life was for me. Wendy's mom asked me to pray with her, and that night I accepted the Lord into my life.

I didn't really understand much about God and the gift of a new life. But if Wendy's mom could love me after everything I'd done, then I knew there is more to Jesus Christ than just knowing who He is.

My own will at first rejected Jesus Christ, but the Holy Spirit gave me the courage, strength, and even the desire to give up drugs and to live for Christ. I thought that if God loves me so much, and if He's willing to make a new person out of me, and give me the power to overcome and resist temptation, how could I lose?

Wendy and I are now married and now look forward to the future with hope for the coming of Christ. I found out last night that the Lord has blessed us with a son. How I thank God for the new life we now have in Jesus. I'm presently serving three to six years for burglary that I committed before I met Christ, but it's been a real blessing. The Lord has given me this time to grow, to study, and to learn more of Him, and His ways. He's also given me this time to serve Him and work for Him.

14. INSTANT EVERYTHING

by Nina Walter

"Barry!" I exclaimed. "How good to see you! Come in and sit down."

The tall young man who had paused in the doorway of my office in Los Angeles City College moved to the chair beside my desk.

"I haven't seen you since. . . ."

"Since I dropped out of school last year," he supplied as I paused. "I know."

Remembering Barry as he had been a year before, I felt a vague hurt. He was thin, and premature lines marked his sallow face. He smiled at me with his mouth, but not with his eyes. I had been his counselor, but he had never asked my advice except in academic matters. Yet we had talked. Intelligent and highly articulate, Barry had been one of my favorite students in English class. Then he had disappeared.

"Tell me about your year," I invited.

He sighed. "I thought I was on the road to a wonderful future. I thought I had found a way to get instant results."

"What kind of results?"

"Instant expansion of my mind, instant deepening of my awareness, instant freedom to do my own thing, instant everything!" he said.

I looked dubious. "How?"

"Through drugs," Barry admitted. "First marijuana. Then LSD, speed, and heroin twice. For a while, I thought I had it made."

"What happened?"

Barry looked down, then looked me in the eye, then dropped his gaze to the floor again. "I — I met myself coming back."

I didn't quite grasp that, but it was obvious that Barry was badly shaken. I pushed some papers around on my desk and waited. Finally he continued.

"My pal Jake, who turned on a year ahead of me, had the same big ideas. He hit the road for a while. Now he's back."

As Barry paused, my memory punched out a file card on Jake — intelligent, willful like Barry, but as unstable as quicksilver.

"How is Jake?" I asked.

"He's a wreck. He has T.B. and V.D. and little crawly things that he doesn't even care about. He looks and acts like a skid row bum."

I gave an exclamation of concern.

"And that isn't all," Barry continued. "He blew his mind. I mean, he really blew it. Sometimes he lies around in a stupor, and sometimes he beats his head against the wall. Yesterday he was taken to the state hospital for the insane, in handcuffs and leg irons."

I pushed my papers around again. A man does not like to be watched while he weeps for a friend. Barry left the chair and walked to the window. For

Instant Everything • 121

a while he stared at the students walking back and forth across the campus. When he came back, his eyes were dry.

"I guess I knew all along there was no easy road to instant everything," he said. "I just tried to kid myself."

"And now?"

"Now I want to drop back in and work at something that promises a real future."

"It's not going to be easy," I warned.

"I know that," Barry replied. "First I have to get the monkey off my back. Then I need the patience and self-discipline to get 'everything' the slow, reliable way. With God's help, I believe I can do it. Will you let me try?"

"We certainly will," I said, speaking for the school. "Drop in now and then and tell me how things are going." As he walked out I offered a silent prayer for the strength he was going to need.

That was four years ago. Barry finished his junior college and went on to state college, planning to become a teacher. He has made a new life for himself. How did he manage to make it back from the drug world of no return? "I was a fallen-away Christian when I became a drug user," Barry says, "and my first step toward rehabilitation was to return to God and to the life of an active, practicing Christian."

15. SPEED WAY TO DESTRUCTION

by Jani Jansen*

Looking through the supermarket window that day in the late 1960s, I saw Slade running from a place the cops were raiding. A quick glance told my too-experienced eyes that he was dehydrating from a heavy dose of speed. His muscles were cramping, and he needed salt. Leaving my bag of groceries, I ran down the aisle of the store, grabbed some salt, and headed for the door. "Someone needs help," I yelled at the startled checking clerk as I ran past.

Three blocks away, Slade and I collapsed on some shaded church steps. Slade forced the salt down as I dashed to a gas station for water. Within fifteen minutes the ordeal was over — for this time.

It had all started six years earlier when I was eighteen. I was part of the "in crowd" at a high school on the West Coast but things didn't move fast enough for me. I was bored and looking for something — anything — more exciting. Drinking became my first "answer."

During college, I remember one morning pulling myself out of bed in a fog. The refrigerator was

---

*Real name withheld on request.

Speed Way to Destruction • 123

empty. There was nothing to drink anywhere. In a panic, I ran to the neighbors. Finally some friends found me enough alcohol to steady my nervous frame. One of them said, "Jani, you can't exist without it." As he said the words I realized I was an alcoholic.

Using the last of my savings, I entered a state mental hospital as a volunteer withdrawal case. During my third month there I met Rod, a manic depressive. He had been a successful student until, unknown to him, someone slipped him an LSD tablet. Now he was pushing heavy drugs to patients in the hospital. As a result, I entered the hospital as an alcoholic and left as an acid-head, or LSD user.

Shortly after being released, I went to southwest Portland to a hippie hangout. Someone asked me if I wanted to try speed. I said No. About fifteen guys surrounded me. "Come on, Jani," one of them teased, "we'll mainline it." He pulled up my sleeve and applied a tourniquet. By then I was ready to go along anyhow. He missed the vein and hit a muscle. The sting was as if a dozen bees had converged on my arm. He tried again. In minutes my body was experiencing tintillating sensations. I bounded out the door up to my apartment, my energy overflowing. Speed became my love, and my apartment became a speed hangout.

Once, after a fourteen-day speed trip, I entered my apartment to find it full of people. Across the room a pair of large black eyes met mine. I asked the girl next to me who he was. "That's Slade, but he's married." OK, so hands off, I thought. I

124 • UNHOOKED

then asked where the speed was. "Slade has some," she said; "he's a pusher."

As my affair with speed continued I began to lose contact with reality. For three weeks I locked myself in a room with only a syringe and a large supply of speed. Somebody finally got me out and took me to an apartment for a few days until some of the drug left my system. Another time I sat for seven days on a couch staring into space, neither eating nor drinking. The only time I got up was to change records.

In order to get drugs, I would steal, cheat, and lie. Cheap living conditions meant crowded apartments and cockroaches. Sick as I was of this type of living, I couldn't stop. I experienced barbiturate poisoning, Methedrine poisoning, mass hallucinations, and "freak outs." My life became like that of an animal. It was under those conditions that I saw Slade run past the market that day and went to his side.

After that, Slade said, "Come on, Jani, I'm taking you with me to the beach." On the way down I asked for a shot of speed. "No more speed," he said, "we're getting off drugs."

A small beach town where no one knew either of us became our home as we both tried to break the grip of drugs. Having Slade with me gave me strength to resist. However, there was one condition we made about quitting drugs. If we ever got our hands on some pure Desoxyn, we would take it. This pure form of speed was rare and very expensive. Finally the day came when Slade brought home the precious morsel. By the time we had used it, Slade had decided to go back to speed. I soon joined him. Our heroic attempt to leave the drug scene had backfired. Slade went back to his wife and I switched to a new kick, Satan worship.

I got in with a girl who had been in the witch thing for a long time. She was responsible to Elji, a demon of destruction. I too was to become his follower. It was exciting and brought me a sense of power. It also enabled me to stay off drugs.

I remember my first black mass, a mockery of the Roman Catholic mass. It included chants and perverted sex acts and climaxed with a sacrifice to Satan in which a girl named Jan burned her baby alive. (I know this seems incredible, but we felt it was only right that we should do what our supreme and all-powerful ruler, Satan, asked.)

I was up for approval before Satan that night. I was told that when I died I would become a demon and could possess people, providing of course that I qualified in every way for Satan's service. Oh, how I wanted to please him.

My assignment in life was to destroy people. My witch taught me that drugs were one of the best tools for this purpose, but there were a lot of other subtle ways to get to people's minds.

Somehow, I awoke one morning with a revulsion for the whole Satan bit. I chucked the witchcraft and took up heroin. I also started riding with a motorcycle gang called the Gypsy Jokers. My urge to destroy was not at all easy to lay aside, and I found myself enjoying the Jokers' escapades of beating helpless people and raping girls.

I had long since realized a tremendous emptiness inside. Nothing, however grotesque or wild, satisfied that deep boredom. I had often thought,

"What do I live for?" Now I progressed to thoughts of suicide, and then to attempts at suicide.

One January morning I started out with eight barbiturates in my pocket. If I didn't find something I was going to mainline them, a sure kill. In the cold snow I walked the streets of Portland. My old jeans had worn white; these and my tee shirt and sandals were not much protection against the north wind. I crossed to a gas station. I planned to shoot the barbiturates in the rest room.

"Jani," someone called. I turned and saw that it was Slade. He had learned of my plans. "I'm taking you to your home, Jani," he said.

There my parents made a last desperate attempt to help me. They called Bill and Margaret Hansell. Margaret had been my closest friend in high school. She and her husband, Bill, were working with a Christian organization. It had been three years since we had seen each other.

In early February 1969 I arrived in Sacramento at Bill and Margaret's comfortable apartment near a college. After I slept for fifteen hours and had some food, Margaret and I sat down for a talk. I pulled up my sleeves to reveal the ugly story of what had happened since we last saw each other. Meshy yellow and black bruises covered both arms. Veins shot too often with heroin were infected and threatened to collapse. The sight was too much for Margaret. She burst into tears, exclaiming, "But Jani, you didn't have to go through all this. It was so unnecessary! God has a much better life for you if you'll just take it."

And now comes the big pitch about Christianity, I thought. Christianity equals church, rules, confinement, authority, I thought. Before Margaret could say anything else I told her, "I've been to church and tried it all. Christianity is for people like you and Bill, but not for me."

Even though I was prepared for a pitch about Christianity, what she said next caught me off guard. "Jani, Christianity is not a religion. Christianity is Jesus Christ."

For twenty minutes Margaret told me about a personal relationship with Jesus Christ. This was new to me. I thought God was distant and inaccessible. Margaret talked as if she knew God . . . as if He were a part of her. When she finished, she handed me a current translation of the New Testament.

Then, on Wednesday, Margaret and Bill invited me to a College Life meeting. My emotions were mixed. What if I didn't fit in? Would they want to know about my past? Without a fix, I didn't see how I could endure it. But finally I consented to go.

Before long I was laughing and singing with the students. I felt so comfortable with them. Then, some of the students stood and shared what God was doing in their lives. Toward the end they sang a song. One of the phrases really hit me: "Then I knew that He was more than just a God who didn't care, who lived away up there." I watched their faces. They sang as if they meant it.

Thursday passed without much happening except at times I tried to piece the puzzle together. Margaret had given me material to read. It told of God's love for the world but that we were independent of it and needed to come back to Him. Jesus Christ, who was God, had actually come to this earth to bring us back into relationship with Him.

128 • UNHOOKED

It made sense to me that God would do this, but somehow I didn't feel it applied to me.

Friday evening Margaret and Bill left me alone for a while and I headed for the phone to make a long distance call to Slade. But as I passed the hall mirror a strange thing happened. I expected the awful physical reflection — the deep, circled eyes, the small, sickly frame — but what made me aghast was what I saw inside. My utter emptiness stood out at first glance. I moved away from the mirror but could not erase the panic that glance had aroused. I suddenly realized how desperately I needed help.

Instinctively, I grabbed for the pamphlet Margaret had given me.

Carefully, I went once again through the pamphlet checking every verse with the Bible. One had Christ saying, "Listen, I stand at the door to your life and knock. If any man will hear My voice and open the door, I will come into him."

After I read the verse, my feelings came tumbling out. "God, I don't want to get busted. I guess I'm desperate. I don't know if You can help me but I'm going to give You a try. I want You to come into my life."

The immediate result of my prayer was a deep sense of forgiveness. Also, I knew somehow that there was a heaven and someday I would be there.

A few days later while reading Margaret's Bible I noticed a verse underlined: "If anyone is in Christ he is a new creation, old things pass away and all things become new." This is what I wanted more than anything — to be a new creation.

"I'm putting you to a test, Lord. If You can't

make me a new person, I'm gonna chuck Christianity."

Within the next few weeks one thing stood out distinctly. I lost my appetite for drugs. Gradually, reality began replacing fantasy. A new inner strength enabled me to face life in a way I never had before. For the first time it was possible to love unselfishly. Christianity began to make sense — real Christianity as it's told in the Bible. The amazing thing was that all this happened without any conscious effort on my part.

A couple of years have passed. My body has not fully recovered. I can't take much pressure; I require lots of sleep, vitamins, and rest. There have been some terrible ordeals. Slade shot himself. He lingered for months, gradually deteriorating. Though he finally accepted Christ, it was too late for him to live for Him here on earth. I was by his side when he died.

All my other close friends in the drug scene have either committed suicide or entered mental institutions. It has taken all the power of the grace of God plus the loving support of many Christians to keep me together. I still have a long, long way to go, but God has given me hope. That's more than any of my former friends have.

16. STEP BY STEP—DOWN

as told to Dorothy Grunbock Johnston

If you were to ask me about the most beautiful thing I possess, I wouldn't hesitate to tell you that apart from being on speaking terms with God because of what His Son did, it's a *sound mind*. I mean being able to think clearly and to come to right conclusions and to make decisions is just the greatest!

It hasn't always been that way. I'm just sixteen now, but when I was in junior high, in the seventh grade, I began a life pattern that led me step by step on a self-destroying binge. Sneaking bourbon and wine from a friend's parents' cupboard was the beginning. Smoking marijuana, taking speed and cough syrup in excess, until my whole being shrieked for more and more, was the end, almost. And when my mind began to go, I was scared, real scared. All this took place before my fifteenth birthday.

My folks didn't know what was going on, of course, because we teens can be pretty clever about covering up. But when I couldn't talk coherently, they thought I was going out of my mind and began to be alarmed. They had more reason to be alarmed than they could possibly know.

Step by Step — Down • 131

Last night in Seattle I went to TeeDruNars — that's short for Teen-age Drug and Narcotics Rehabilitation — because it was Monday, and every Monday and Thursday evening from 7 to 10:30 is reserved for this. Actually, visitors aren't welcome and aren't even allowed to sit in on our sessions unless the group votes OK. But if you'd been there, you might not have even noticed a very small girl, with long straight red hair and granny glasses, wearing a bright yellow sweater and socks to match, and jeans. But it was me. I've always been shy and still am. That's why I try to sit back of the circle of forty kids or so who gather to hassle about the problems they are facing since they have decided to go off drugs.

One fellow's hair is long and wavy and from the back you might even think it was a girl sitting there. The other fellows wear their hair in varying lengths and some look like the clean-cut kid type, and just to look at them, you'd wonder what they were doing there. But when they open their mouths, you know they are familiar with the drug scene. There are girls, too, but not as many as there are boys. Each of us recognizes what drugs were doing to his body, to his mind, to his outlook on life, to his future, and has made the decision to stop using drugs entirely. His being there at TeeDruNars is actually a cry for help. And help is what we give each other. Moral support, you might say. Each one lends a sympathetic ear and everyone knows he can depend on another to give the same when he needs it — because we all have our good and bad days. Quitting dope isn't easy any way you look at it.

Maybe you're wondering how I got started in the

132 • UNHOOKED

first place. Ours is an average middle-class American home, I'd say. Dad is a salesman. Mom has taken me and my brother, four years younger than I, to Sunday School for as long as I can remember. But somehow the *personal* aspect of Christianity was never explained so it hit home.

And because I was shy and desperately longed to be noticed and to have friends and be accepted by the "in" group, I readily accepted the challenge to try the things many parents frown on for kids but seem to think is OK for themselves. Because my mother works, it was no problem to go home with a girl friend and sample bourbon and wine from her parents' supply. In our suburban section there are wooded areas, perfect places to smoke unnoticed. This we did. In the ninth grade, my generous friend offered me marijuana. She was a year older and had a driver's license and worked in a nearby rest home which meant she had plenty of money and a car. So getting the stuff and finding a secluded spot to try it was no problem.

At first, the dizzy feeling I had when I smoked pot was fascinating. When it made my mind go blank, I was immune to what was going on; it seemed like there weren't any problems. So during the summer, instead of sneaking off a couple of times a month for a reefer, my friend and I were going to the woods or to the beach quite a lot. It was then that my folks noticed my incoherent speech and became alarmed.

To get me away from this friend, I was sent to live with my grandmother in Seattle. But you can't walk down University Way without some pusher hissing, "Speed, acid, pot," at you. And if you are in the market for one of these, the transaction takes place. High school- and college-aged drug users were quick to spot the fact that I was willing to be one of them and I had invitations to listen to records at their pads. Speed and cough syrup (which has Dexedrine or codeine in it) were still supplied by that friend.

To add insult to injury, I was enrolled by my parents in a Christian school. I was furious and I was bitter. Cut off from my drug-supplying friend, I wasn't able to smoke pot. This made me more bitter and uncooperative.

One weekend I went home and it was then that my mother went to Grandma's and searched my room. In a drawer she found a bag of weed. She suspected it was marijuana but wasn't sure. A call to a pastor who had studied the subject brought him to inspect my room. Various signs caused him to tell my mother that she had a dope user as a daughter.

The next day I was taken to that church to talk to the pastor. I was amazed to meet up with a *preacher* who knew more about dope than I did. Because of this, he knew everything about me before I opened my mouth. He advised my parents to disown me. Sound drastic? It had to be that way. I had to see that I couldn't expect my parents to support a dope addict. I slept on the couch in the lounge at church that night. The next two nights were spent in the pastor's home. And all that time everyone was waiting for me to decide if I would continue on dope or rejoin the human race *without drugs*. It was up to me.

I must say that my mind was in a muddle and I

134 • UNHOOKED

didn't know what I wanted. But a visit Monday night to TeeDruNar made me decide to go straight. It was the turning point for me.

For thirteen months, now, I've been going twice a week. Sharing my feelings and temptations with others in the same boat helps me. And I am able, in turn, to help others. A new boy came last night because I invited him. I made the coffee. And when they needed a new board member to discuss the plans and policies, I was elected. I may be shy, but I want to help other kids who are in the same muddled state I once was.

But the important part of my story is the fact that I don't have to fight this drug thing alone. Almost a year ago, a girl at the Christian school my father sent me to told me how she used to drink and how being saved had changed her life. After English class was over we sat and talked a long time. Of course, teachers and counselors had taken advantage of opportunities to tell their students how Christ had died to take the punishment for our sins. I knew what Christ had done for me and I knew what I had to do to make Him mine. But I just hadn't come to the deciding point. Now this girl's story about the change knowing the Lord Jesus Christ had made in her, intrigued me. On the bus on the way home from school that day, I asked Jesus to become *my* Saviour. And He did. Now I have Christian friends.

And once in a while I am asked to be part of a team that goes to a school, a PTA, youth group or some other gathering to talk for a few minutes about the "before" and "after" aspects of being on drugs.

My parents attend Naranon, a place where parents of kids like me discuss *their* problems. I guess I was pretty selfish in what I did, not caring about my parents or their concern for me.

I might say that a lot of kids turn to dope because they feel they aren't loved. They become wrapped up in themselves instead of caring about others. We need to show love and concern. And we need to tell them about the greatest love of all, Christ's love.

Dope is a hard crutch to give up because it becomes so much a part of you, or rather you become so much a part of it. Dope certainly takes you over and controls your life so that you are no longer the person you were meant to be when God created you.

But now I'm free of it and I am grateful. Like I said, apart from knowing God in a personal way, the most beautiful thing I have is a *sound mind!*

17. JUST ONE MORE

by Parker Rice as told to Muriel Larson

"Your father's a Bible thumper!" jeered one of my friends. "And you'll probably be a lily-livered Bible thumper youself!"

"I will not!" I declared angrily. I didn't realize that with that declaration I was turning away from God. "I'll show you who's a Bible thumper. I can do anything you can do — and more!" And I set out to prove it.

I was fourteen years old and I didn't want to be called "preacher's kid" or "Bible thumper." I wanted to be one of the fellows.

And many of the kids on my street in Greenville, South Carolina, smoked, cursed, drank, and sniffed glue. My mother had a job. So she wasn't there when I came home from school. I was free to do what I wanted. I started living my new life by skipping school, smoking cigars, and using profanity. From that I "graduated" to drinking and glue sniffing.

Dad found out about it and punished me. I argued with my parents, disobeyed them, and in general made life rough. My new way of living had really created a "generation gap" between me and my parents!

Just One More • 137

"Listen, Parker, you don't have to take that stuff from your father," one of my buddies told me. "Why don't you run away?" So I did. Another friend who was dissatisfied with home ran away with me. But after three days I phoned Dad and he promised me I wouldn't be punished. So I went home.

Shortly after that my parents discovered I had flunked tenth grade at Carolina High School. Naturally they were upset and angry with me. So in June 1969 I ran away again.

In Atlanta I stayed at a hippie crash pad for a week. I drank a lot and had my first marijuana cigarette. I steered clear of other drugs at that time, however, because I was still scared of them. Since my dad had been the assistant director of a rescue mission for six years, I was well acquainted with the dangers involved in drug taking.

From Atlanta I hitchhiked down to Florida. I lived off the handouts of truck drivers. I was just a bum now. I got picked up by the St. Augustine police. They notified my parents and my father sent me a bus ticket back to Greenville. I took the bus — but got off at Atlanta and returned to the hippie pad.

Then I got what I thought was a good idea. I told a hippie acquaintance, "I have some friends out in Texas. I think I'll hitchhike out there and visit them. Will they be surprised to see me!"

They certainly *would* be surprised. When I had lived in McAllen, Texas, on the border of Mexico, my parents had worked as missionaries with the Mexicans. I had always been a clean-cut fellow.

138 • UNHOOKED

Now my hair was long and I was a smoking, drinking, swearing, glue-sniffing hippie!

I bummed my way across the country sixteen hundred miles to McAllen, mostly by hitchhiking. "Parker Rice!" exclaimed one of my old friends, Albert, when he saw me. "You ain't no preacher's kid no more, are you?" Albert had never been particularly good himself.

I stayed in McAllen a week, taking marijuana, inhaling Freon, and even trying peyote with Albert and another friend. Then I hitchhiked to New Orleans, where they were having a pop festival. There were thirty-three thousand people there, and you could get anything you wanted — wine, liquor, LSD, marijuana, and heroin were being used freely.

After listening to psychedelic music for twelve hours, you lose control of your mind. Getting drunk and smoking marijuana didn't help either. It was at this festival I first took LSD.

Then I got picked up by the New Orleans police who made sure I got home. Dad met my plane in Atlanta, and the first thing he did when I got home was to cut off my hair. I went back to the tenth grade in September, but only stayed straight for a few weeks. Back I went to glue sniffing. I also got my brothers started on it, for which I'm very sorry now. Glue sniffing is psychologically addictive and destroys your brain cells!

Then I heard of a pop festival taking place right in Greenville. I attended and took some more LSD. From there I went to Atlanta, where I took LSD, mescaline, hash, speed, and other drugs. During the next nine months I left home four or five times and took more than fifty "trips" on LSD. I had quit school after the first three weeks back in Greenville. I had sworn at a teacher, sassed the principal, turned on my heel, and walked out.

While I was hitchhiking down to New Orleans for the Mardi Gras, I was again picked up by the police. I had four days in jail with nothing to do but think. How empty my life is, I thought. *I've lost all control of myself! What a fool I've been!*

"Lord," I prayed, "please straighten my life out. I turn it over to You." When I told the sheriff of my change of heart, he let me go so I could return home. I really wanted to change. I even got my hair cut. But when I got to Atlanta I weakened.

I thought, *Just one more trip won't hurt.* But that did it. I was back in slavery again, helpless. After staying in Atlanta for a while, I finally returned to Greenville — but I didn't go home. I lived on the streets and with the hippies.

Then one day I was riding around with some friends. The driver was high on morphine. We stopped to try to get some money to buy more morphine, but when we couldn't get any, the driver took off angrily — without me!

When someone looked at the speedometer of his wrecked car later, it was stuck at 115 mph. The five fellows and girls who had been in the car were badly injured and in the hospital. As I sat across the street from the hospital where my friends were, I thought, *What a narrow escape I had. I ought to go home.*

I did go home, but I continued taking drugs. Then one day in February 1970, my parents told me about a former drug addict, Domingo Garcia, who was going to speak at Morningside Baptist

Church. They urged me to go and hear him. So I did, two nights in a row. That second night I talked to Domingo after the service. I told him, "I've tried to get off drugs, but for me it's just impossible."

He answered, "Parker, you give God a chance in your life and if He does not change you, I will throw away my Bible and stop preaching!"

The following night I brought five of my hippie friends to the service. At first they giggled, laughed, and blasphemed the singing. Then when Domingo started speaking, they grew quiet. At the close of the service we all walked to the altar to turn our lives over to the Lord. I had thought I was saved before, but everything was so muddled in my mind. I just had to get right with the Lord.

Some of the fellows have gone back to their former way of life. It's hard to give up drugs when you're surrounded by temptation. But Domingo started a rehabiliation center for addicts in Travelers Rest, South Carolina, and I was his first "customer." He keeps addicts there for six months, filling them with a knowledge of the Lord and the Bible.

Although I had made some sort of "decision" when I was young, I feel that Christ really came into my heart and life that night I walked the aisle. Now I find my daily Bible reading gives me strength and joy. The Lord has taken away the desire for drugs and has planted a new desire in my heart — to serve Him.

Now instead of carrying drugs, I carry my Bible. I want to be a man of God just like my dad! I feel the only way I can possibly make up to my parents for all the terrible heartache I have caused them is to live all out for the Lord.

The drugs I had been on for so long had affected my eyesight and my mind. But the Lord has given me a new heart, and I now realize I was nothing but a dirty bum! But with God's help I'm going to live for Him. Now I'm attending Greenville Technical Education Center in order to get my high school certificate. And soon I hope to be able to attend my dad's *alma mater* — Bob Jones University here in Greenville.

"He brought me up also out of an horrible pit, out of the miry clay, and set my feet upon a rock and established my goings" (Ps. 40:2).

18. HOW TO SPOT A DRUG USER

Getting ready for an appointment for a new family portrait for their prayer cards, a mother in a missionary family home on furlough from a foreign field, suggested to fourteen-year-old Sally that she hurry to change into different clothes. Normally a cooperative, lovable girl, Sally stubbornly refused and cried and began wringing her hands. Then she sat down and began laughing.

Anxious about their daughter's unusual behavior, the parents had cause for further alarm that evening at a birthday party when Sally's conversation became garbled.

Two days later Sally became completely irrational. Her eyes rolled or stared blankly; her speech made no sense. When her mother asked if Sally knew her, she replied, "I'm *your* mother."

After Sally was admitted to a hospital, doctors immediately suspected she had somehow gotten hold of a drug. But her parents refused to believe a girl as sweet and innocent as Sally could be involved in the drug scene. Sally remained in a coma-like state for four days before beginning to improve. In time, after talking with Sally and several of her junior high schoolmates, the parents concluded that someone had drugged her. "Some kids last year in the lunch

How to Spot a Drug User • 143

room were dropping LSD into other kids' pop," a school friend revealed. "They wanted to see others take trips." Apparently Sally had been a victim of an LSD practical joker.

If Sally's parents had been plugged in on the drug scene, they likely would have suspected drugs prior to rushing her to the hospital. They could be excused, having been out of the country when the drug problem hit. But parents who have remained here at home should not be so easily caught off guard when a child falls victim to drugs.

Keen observation and a knowledge of what drugs do to change a young person are vital in order to possibly nip the problem in the bud and take steps to help.

"A lot of parents who have children with drug problems will take the time to play golf or garden, but the parents won't set one evening aside to acquire the knowledge they really need," says Dr. Donald B. Louria, author of two books on drugs, the latest being *Overcoming Drugs*.

Entertainer Art Linkletter, whose twenty-year-old daughter, Diane, died in October 1969 in a suicide plunge blamed on LSD, laments the fact he didn't know enough about the drug scene.

In a *Chicago Tribune Magazine* article titled "What I Learned Too Late About Dope," he said, "We have been as unequipped to handle this thing as the college presidents have been to handle riots. Just as they have all fallen back and regrouped and compared experiences and decided on policies, so parents should be doing that today."

Since Diane's death Linkletter has toured the country speaking to parents and youths about the danger of drug abuse. (He also introduces "High on the Campus," a film that seeks to combat drug use among junior and senior high students, released by Gospel Films, Muskegon, Mich.) He wishes he had been aware of the overwhelming force of peer group pressure and had given more attention to the older friends with whom his daughter associated.

When people call him in panic and say, "I think my kid is on something," he says: "Well, look at her friends. What kind of people are they? Where do they go? What do they talk about? Do you know?" Linkletter hastens to add that, despite the fact her friends are weird or otherwise undesirable, "you can't say, 'I'm going to wipe out all your friends.'" He recommends long talks without scolding and reprimanding — talks giving the feeling that you're a friend who's standing by no matter what happens.

Lon Gregg, who tells his story in this book, has helpful suggestions. "Watch for young people whose spending habits, use of free time, care in appearance, or sense of well-being show sudden or drastic variation: they may well be experimenting with drugs. Even an embarrassingly frank interview with the young person in question may be worthwhile to find out exactly what transpires at school, at the neighborhood drive-in, or any other place where the youngster gathers with friends."

Marijuana smokers can often be detected by a burnt-rope-like odor on the breath and clothing, according to Dr. T. R. Van Dellen, *Chicago Tribune* columnist. "The effects of marijuana seldom offer any clues unless the user is observed soon after the cigarette is smoked," Van Dellen continues. "Stimu-

How to Spot a Drug User

lation is the immediate effect. The user looks hysterical and becomes vivacious, talking rapidly and loudly. Later, he becomes sleepy and somewhat stuporous."

Dr. Hardin Jones, of Berkeley (quoted in the Introduction) gives parents eight tips to aid them in recognizing a possible drug user:

"1. Marijuana produces redness of the eyes. Some drugs cause dilation or constriction of pupils. The facts that youngsters get red-eyed easily from lack of sleep, too, and that they have wide pupils when they are not out in the sunlight make these symptoms uncertain by themselves.

"2. Some drugs produce drowsiness and clumsiness. Since most normal young people don't bump into things often, these may be signs of trouble.

"3. Marijuana and LSD commonly produce abrupt changes in goals and work habits. Those who have the hardest drive for goals and performance seem to be the most affected. This is an important clue, but youngsters are changeable for many normal reasons also.

"4. Know the smell of marijuana smoke and the appearance of 'grass.' Your police department can arrange for you to recognize this evidence. The smell is hard to hide; at illicit pot parties, there is often an attempt to cover the characteristic sweet odor by burning incense. Therefore, burning incense is often a clue.

"5. If your youngster is reported to be nude in a public place or to be generally incoherent, he is possibly intoxicated with LSD.

"6. A succession of disappearances of articles of value from your household would be reason to suspect that someone with access to things has become addicted to hard drugs.

"7. Diet pills are usually composed of one of the amphetamines. Drug users often take a number of pills at a time for the mental intoxication sought. An amphetamine user has an abnormal feeling of power. He is easily triggered into violence.

"8. Barbiturates are the active substances in most sleeping pills. They are currently being used on a massive scale to induce intoxication. Their chief symptom is drowsiness."

Dr. Jones reminds that you are more likely to pick up information about drug use by other families' children than about your own. "If so, you have an urgent obligation to see that those parents are informed quickly, privately, and confidentially," he asserts.

A U.S. Government Printing Office pamphlet, "Has Anyone You Care About Changed for No Apparent Reason?" gives suggestions to aid in helping recognize a drug user. Has there been a change. . . .

". . . From clear, talkative, expressive to silent, confused, withdrawn?

". . . From vital, healthy, energetic to nervous, up-tight, restless?

". . . From poised, confident, self-assured to oppressed, tormented, persecuted?

". . . From helpful, attentive, dependable to vague, forgetful, disinterested?

". . . From eager, active, enthusiastic to passive, apathetic, hopeless?

". . . From open, friendly, trusting to suspicious, antagonistic, alienated?

". . . From cheerful, optimistic, pleasant to cynical, pessimistic, moody?"

Where does one go to find help for a loved one who has been hooked on drugs? A physician or minister could help find the best resource in the community. As pointed out in the Introduction and as reflected in the stories themselves, Christian agencies offer help that has been proved to work time after time. (See listing that follows.) The power of Jesus Christ, introduced to addicts by Christians in the front line in the fight against the drug problem, can mean the difference between life and death . . . between being hooked for life and being unhooked!

HELP FOR ADDICTS

Across the United States and Canada scores of centers and agencies offer a helping hand to drug addicts and prescribe a cure through a personal encounter with Jesus Christ. In addition, pastors of evangelical, Bible-believing churches stand ready to counsel drug users and point them to the One who can fill the void in their lives. Teen-agers can find help through workers associated with such organizations as Youth for Christ (Campus Life), Young Life, Word of Life, and High School Evangelism Fellowship, among youth movements that seek to bring high-schoolers into an abundant kind of life through Christ. Collegians can obtain spiritual counsel from workers associated with such organizations as Campus Crusade for Christ, The Navigators, and Inter-Varsity Christian Fellowship (see p. 154 for addresses of these organizations). In most large cities addicts of all ages will receive excellent spiritual aid by going to a Gospel rescue mission such as Pacific Garden Mission, Chicago; Union Rescue Mission, Los Angeles; Bowery Mission and McAuley Water Street Mission, New York City; Mel Trotter Mission, Grand Rapids; Detroit City Rescue Mission, Detroit; or Memphis Union Mission, Memphis.

Centers and Agencies Specializing in Help for Addicts

(This list was compiled in a spot check of a representative group of evangelical leaders. It does not pretend to be a complete listing of all Christian centers combatting the drug problem.)

Arizona

Phoenix Teen Challenge, 21 W. Willetta, Phoenix 85003

Arkansas

Little Rock Teen Challenge, 1000 W. 55th St., North Little Rock 72118

California

Bakersfield Teen Challenge, 2030 Truxton, Bakersfield 93301

Maranatha House, 60 Union Ave., Campbell 95008

Inland Empire Teen Challenge, 9395 San Bernardino Rd., Cucamonga 91730

Outreach for Youth, 2921 N. Blackstone Ave., Fresno 93703

Christian Anti-Narcotic Association, P.O. Box 946, Hesperia 92345

His Place, 8428 Sunset Blvd., Hollywood 90069

Halfway House (His Place), 1935 S. Oxford Ave., Los Angeles 90018

Los Angeles Teen Challenge, P.O. Box 585, Main Station, Los Angeles 90053

Manhattan Project (Salvation Army), 916 Francisco St., Los Angeles 90015

Shepherd Foundation, P.O. Box 141, Lynwood 90262

Orange County Teen Challenge, 78 Plaza Sq., Orange 92666

Youth Action Center, 704 Garnet (Pacific Beach), San Diego 92109

San Diego Teen Challenge, P.O. Box 4332, North Park Station, San Diego 92104

San Francisco Teen Challenge, 959 S. Van Ness Ave., San Francisco 94109

Drug Abuse Information Service, Inc., 1190 Lincoln Ave., San Jose 95125

Maranatha House, 1340 Sharp Ave., San Jose 95124

Young Life (Paul Schilperoot), 434 E. William St., Suite A, San Jose 95112

Help for Addicts • 151

Frank Gonzales Evangelistic Association, 9601 San Carlos, South Gate 90280

Colorado

Denver Teen Challenge, 3225 Wyandot, Denver 80211

Florida

House of Ichthus, 2391 Wilton Dr., Ft. Lauderdale 33305

Turning Point Halfway House, 400 S.W. 2 St., Pompano Beach 33060

Turning Point, 2600 N.W. 112 St., Miami 33167

Young Life (Charles Scott), 359 E. Fairbanks St., Winter Park 32789

Georgia

Teen Challenge of Georgia, 40 14th St., N.E., Atlanta 30309

Girls Lodge (Salvation Army), 127 11th St., N.E., Atlanta 30309

Illinois

Prevention, Inc., 1336 N. Hoyne, Chicago 60622

Chicago Teen Challenge, 315 S. Ashland Ave., Chicago 60607

Young Life (George Sheffer), 727 N. Oak St., Hinsdale 60521

Indiana

Indianapolis Teen Challenge, 145 E. Fall Creek Parkway, S., Indianapolis 46205

Massachusetts

Boston Teen Challenge, 1315 Main St., Brockton 02401

Michigan

Detroit Teen Challenge, 4600 Lovett, Detroit 48210

Missouri

St. Louis Teen Challenge, P.O. Box 4915, Field Station, St. Louis 63108

152 • UNHOOKED

New Jersey

Ambassadors for Christ, 27 N. 17th St., East Orange 07017

Central Jersey Teen Challenge, 646 Broadway, Long Branch 07740

Teen Challenge, 39 Broadway, Paterson 07505

New York

Love Inn, 1768 Dryden Rd., Freeville 13068

Correctional Service for Women (Salvation Army), 545 Avenue of the Americas, New York 10011

COP Outreach Program (Salvation Army), 1991 Lexington Ave., New York 10035

Crossroads Center (Youth Development, Inc.), 230 E. 105th St., Hell Gate Station, New York 10029

New York Teen Challenge, 444 Clinton Ave., Brooklyn, New York 11238

Stuyvesant Square Center (Salvation Army), Women's Narcotic Treatment Program, 231-35 E. 17th St., New York 10003

Young Life (Clark Jones), P.O. Box 273, Knickerbocker Sta., New York 10002

Rochester Teen Challenge, 73 Alexander St., Rochester 14620

Ohio

Cleveland Teen Challenge, Hanna Bldg., Cleveland 44115

Columbus Teen Challenge, 47 E. 12th Ave., Columbus 43201

Exodus Center, 1315 Dennison Ave., Columbus 43201

Outreach for Youth, 422 Chittenden Ave., Columbus 43201

Grace Haven Ranch, Rt. 5, Woodville Rd., Mansfield 44903

Oklahoma

Oklahoma City Teen Challenge, 33 S.W. 25th St., Oklahoma City 73109

Help for Addicts • 153

Oregon

Maranatha Evangelistic Center, 1222 N.E. Skidmore St., Portland 97211

Pennsylvania

Harrisburg Teen Challenge, 1421 N. Front, Harrisburg 17102

Philadelphia Teen Challenge, 1620 N. Broad St., Philadelphia 19121

Teen Haven, 1911 Mount Vernon St., Philadelphia 19130

Hope for the Addict, Inc., 7921 Frankstown Ave., Pittsburgh 15221

Pittsburgh Teen Challenge, 3035 Perrysville Ave., Pittsburgh 15214

Teen Tab., Inc., Pittsburgh Life Bldg., Pittsburgh 15222

Youth Guidance, Inc., Suite 600, 100 Fifth Avenue Bldg., Pittsburgh 15222

Rhode Island

City and Town Missions, 6400 Post Rd., North Kingstown 02852

South Carolina

South Carolina Teen Challenge, 128 Main St., Travelers Rest 29690

Texas

Dallas Teen Challenge, P.O. Box 26112, Fair Park Station, Dallas 75226

Fort Worth Teen Challenge, 110 N. Commerce, Fort Worth 76102

Houston Teen Challenge, 519 Sul Ross, Houston 77006

Young Life (Brent Johnson), P.O. Box 13004, Houston 77019

Austin Teen Challenge, 603 Margo, Longview 75601

San Antonio Teen Challenge, P.O. Box 2242, San Antonio 78206

154 • UNHOOKED

Washington
Conquest House, 19204 15th N.E., Seattle 98155
Grapevine Shelter, 424 S. 152nd St., Seattle 98148
Seadrunar, 809 15th Ave., E., Seattle 98102
Seattle Teen Challenge, 1821 17th Ave., Seattle 98122

Washington, D.C.
Teen Haven, 1430 Newton St., N.W. 20010
Washington, D.C. Teen Challenge, P.O. Box 6165 20044
Youth Unlimited, 1004 Barney Cir., S.E. 20003

Ontario
Toronto Teen Challenge, 658 Broadview Ave., Toronto

British Columbia
Vancouver Teen Challenge, 2360 S.E. Marine Dr., Vancouver

Organizations Whose Workers Often Counsel Youth Addicted to Drugs

High School Organizations
High School Evangelism Fellowship, Inc., P.O. Box 2345, South Hackensack, New Jersey 07606
Word of Life Fellowship, Inc., Schroon Lake, New York 12870
Young Life, 720 W. Monument St., Colorado Springs, Colorado 80904
Youth for Christ, Int., Box 419, Wheaton, Illinois 60187

College Organizations
Campus Crusade for Christ, Int., Arrowhead Springs Hotel, San Bernardino, California 92404
Inter-Varsity Christian Fellowship, 233 Langdon St., Madison, Wisconsin 53703
The Navigators, Colorado Springs, Colorado 80901

ABOUT SOME OF THE WORDS USED IN THIS BOOK

addict: A person psychologically or physically dependent on drugs.

acid: LSD.

acidhead: Frequent user of LSD.

amphetamines: Stimulants, such as "pep pills," "wake-ups," or "bennies." Continued abuse of amphetamines can cause high blood pressure, abnormal heart rhythms, and even may be responsible for severe emotional disturbances, as toxic psychosis or paranoid reactions.

belladonna: A wild plant used as an intoxicant that can cause delirium or death, depending on the amount ingested.

bennies: Benzedrine.
Benzedrine: Stimulant used medically in treatment of obesity, fatigue, or depression. Abuse may cause emotional dependence, resulting in nausea, confusion, irritability.

busted: Arrested.

cold turkey: Breaking the drug habit without medical aid; relates chiefly to physically addicting drugs.

depressant: Barbiturates known to drug abusers as "barbs," "candy," "goofballs," "downers," and other names. Used to induce sleep and relieve stress. Continued and excessive dosages result in slurring of

156 • UNHOOKED

speech, staggering, loss of balance and falling, quick temper, and quarrelsome disposition.

fix: Injection of narcotics or other drugs.

grass: Marijuana.

hallucinogen: Drugs capable of provoking changes of sensation, thinking, self-awareness, and emotion.

hard stuff: Heroin.

hash, hashish: Dark brown resin from the tops of potent *Cannabis sativa* — five times stronger than marijuana.

heroin: Narcotic drug with effect similar to that of morphine. Gives user expanded ego and exaggerated personal value and happiness. Later, it causes user to become antisocial and criminal as he loses sense of pity, remorse, and sense of responsibility. Highly addictive.

high: Under the influence of drugs.

hooked: Addicted psychologically or physically.

junkie: Narcotics addict.

kick the habit: Stop using narcotics (from the withdrawal leg muscle twitches that accompany withdrawal).

LSD: Lysergic acid diethylamide, converted from ergot, the fungus that spoils rye grain. Most potent and best-studied hallucinogen. May produce "good trips" consisting of pleasant imagery and feelings of grandeur or "bad trips" that produce panic reactions.

mainline: Inject drugs into a vein for the quickest reaction.

marijuana: Indian hemp (*Cannabis sativa*) containing tetrahydrocannabinol (THC), believed to be the active ingredient that produces mental effects. Leaves are smoked.

mescaline: The alkaloid in peyote.

methamphetamine: Chemically related to ampheta-

About Some of the Words Used in This Book • 157

mine but acts more directly on the central nervous system and correspondingly less on blood pressure and heart rate. Often called "speed," "crystals," or "meth." Some abusers "shoot" (take intravenously) and may build up to doses of more than one hundred times the medicinal dose, sometimes resulting in an acute toxic state.

narcotics: Generally refers to drugs made from opium, such as heroin, codeine, and morphine.

pop: Inject drugs.

pot: Marijuana.

psychedelics: Hallucinogens.

pusher: Drug peddler.

reefer: Marijuana cigarette.

shooting gallery: Place where addicts inject drugs.

skin popping: Injecting drugs under the skin for speedy reaction.

speed: Methadrine (methamphetamine).

speed freak: User of methamphetamine ("speed") who injects massive doses intravenously once or a dozen times a day, producing practically the same effects as cocaine.

sniff (or **snort**): To inhale a drug for quick results.

stimulant: Group of drugs, including amphetamines, which act on the nervous system.

stoned: Under the strong influence of a drug.

trip: A psychedelic experience. Trips may be "good" or "bad." Instead of pleasant imagery and emotional feelings, the tripper may perceive terrifying images bringing about an emotional state of dread and horror.

weed: Marijuana.

158 • UNHOOKED

Religious terms mentioned

Christian: One who is committed to Christ. By an act of faith he has received Jesus Christ as Saviour from the penalty of sin. This act (and not any righteousness of his own) makes him a member of God's family. "But as many as received him [Jesus] to them gave he the power to become the sons of God, even to them that believed on his name" (John 1:12).

evangelism: Communicating the message of Jesus Christ to others and sharing how they, too, may be forgiven of sin and become Christians.

"Four Spiritual Laws": Simple statement of four Biblical steps that reveal how one may know God's plan for his life, come into a personal relationship with God, and experience an abundant life, as promised by Christ. Widely used by Christians, including many Roman Catholics. Booklet available from Campus Crusade for Christ, Arrowhead Springs Hotel, San Bernardino, Calif. 92404.

Gospel: The good news of the death and resurrection of Christ, which declares that sinners who believe on Christ may be forgiven of their sin and become members of God's family. "I declare unto you the gospel . . . how that Christ died for our sins according to the scriptures; and that he was buried and that he rose again the third day according to the scriptures" (I Cor. 15:1, 3, 4).

Holy Spirit: God's Spirit who indwells every Christian, enabling the believer to live the Christian life. The Holy Spirit gives the power to break sinful habits, including the drug habit. "Walk in the Spirit, and ye shall not fulfil the lust of the flesh" (Gal. 5:16).

Jesus Christ: Very God who became man, not only to live a perfect life, but to become a sacrifice for sin sufficient for forgiveness of the sin of people of all time. (All that is necessary is to believe that He did it for you and commit your life to Him.) He rose from the

About Some of the Words Used in This Book • 159

grave, exhibiting His victory over death and perfecting His earthly work. Only He could declare, as He did, "I am the way, the truth, and the life: no man cometh unto the Father [God] except by me" (John 14:6).

Satan: Spiritual being, archenemy of God and all that is good; head of all evil forces, including demons, that pollute minds and hearts of men. Since God created men capable of making choices, Satan therefore vies with God for the control of individuals. ". . . Turn them from darkness to light, and from the power of Satan unto God, that they may receive forgiveness of sins . . ." (Acts 26:18).

saved: A Biblical term signifying the state of being forgiven of sin and being no longer destined to eternal punishment; to be sure of heaven through faith in Jesus Christ. "What shall I do to be saved? . . . Believe on the Lord Jesus Christ, and thou shalt be saved" (Acts 16:30, 31).

sinner: Anyone — religious or not religious, dope addict or nonaddict. "For all have sinned and come short of the glory of God" (Romans 3:23). Sin itself is basically rebellion against God, whether in hate or murder, giving oneself to drug addiction, being given to selfishly piling up material wealth, or any of a myriad of other manifestations. Simply running one's own life and not giving God His rightful place as Lord of one's life is sin. Christians are forgiven sinners, but sinners battling against sin and with access to the power of the Holy Spirit to keep them from continuing in sin.